BUTTERFLY COOING LIKE A DOVE

Butterfly cooing like a Dove

MIRIAM ROTHSCHILD

Doubleday

NEW YORK · LONDON · TORONTO · SYDNEY · AUCKLAND

PUBLISHED BY DOUBLEDAY
a division of
Bantam Doubleday Dell Publishing Group, Inc.
666 Fifth Avenue, New York, New York 10103

DOUBLEDAY and the portrayal of an anchor with a dolphin
are trademarks of Doubleday,
a division of
Bantam Doubleday Dell Publishing Group, Inc.

Library of Congress Cataloging-in-Publication Data

Rothschild, Miriam.
Butterfly cooing like a dove/
Miriam Rothschild.   1st ed.
p. cm.
Includes index.
1. Butterflies.   2. Butterflies in literature.
3. Columbidae.   4. Doves in literature.
I. Title
QL 544.R67 1991
595.78′9—dc19   89 1267
                                              CIP

ISBN 0-385-26376-7
Copyright © 1991 by Miriam Rothschild
All Rights Reserved
Printed in Italy in 1991
First Edition

For A. and E.

That which hath Wings shall tell the matter.

Contents

List of Plates

x

Foreword

So many friends have taken a kindly interest in this compilation and have offered additions, contributions, comments, criticisms, cries of protest, congratulations, and careful corrections that it would be quite impossible to thank them adequately for their efforts on our behalf. There are one or two willing martyrs whom I feel bound to mention individually and with special gratitude: First is 'E', of the dedication, who relentlessly and affectionately coerced me into print; and second is Pamela Egremont who approved and encouraged my straying from fleas to fancy. Then my daughters Rozsika and Charlotte gave me assistance with the literature on the soul and the spirit; Carmen Wheatley researched many obscure sources, especially the Spanish literature, and made some fine poetic translations; Anna de Egrey provided much information about Spanish tombs, their inscriptions and decoration; Christopher Fry suggested two excellent contributions for the text; Elena Malagodi made several perspicacious suggestions and erasures; Denise Mayer gave valuable and erudite advice on certain French sources; Serena Black and Simon Rendall took infinite pains in preparing and designing the book for publication; the late Alix de Rothschild, Isaiah Berlin and Deidre Clark read and corrected parts or all of the text. I must also extend special thanks to Karl Katz – for one brief moment almost a joint author – who passed the manuscript on to Jacqueline Kennedy Onassis for appraisal and eventual approval.

In addition I would like to express my appreciation of the photographers who made original pictures and excellent reproductions of various works of art and drawings for us: Jean Besancenot, Gene Cox, Robert Cotton, John Hayward, George Lane, Kazuo Unno.

. . . cracked into shining wings

Preface

The reproductions printed in this collection, and the quotations, were assembled in a purely haphazard fashion and merely represent moments of agreeable discovery and the ringing of a chance bell. In particular, a few of the lines of verse and prose were jotted down without reference to their authors or their sources, and I have left them so, since this is a compilation of mood and spontaneous pleasure – it lacks structure, let alone erudition.* But I hope it also demonstrates that one can find considerable enjoyment by mixing up the poetry of words or line with technical facts concerning natural history.

I have encountered one insuperable difficulty: the collection is too large and too varied. Enough material has accumulated over the years to make three or four similar compilations possible. In the end I selected those pictures and quotations that we like best today. Consequently some artists and some writers have been allocated more than their fair share of space. I have one profound regret. The most beautiful moth painting I have ever seen, an Angle Shades asleep on the leaves of an *Agapanthus* in bloom, is stored somewhere in the Imperial Palace in Beijing. I was not allowed to photograph it, nor was I given permission to reproduce it.

Thoreau once remarked that all good science is, in a sense, autobiographical, and I fancy this is true of natural history, and perhaps also of painting and poetry; it is certainly true of this rambling anthology.

*Unless otherwise stated, the translations are by the author.

The Soul's fair emblem

Introduction

One of the secrets of happiness is knowing how to be bored. If you are foolhardy enough to contemplate science as a profession – whether you are a prospective physicist or botanist – you soon realise you must come to terms with boredom. When I was a student at the Marine Biological Station at Plymouth, fate decreed that I should spend a considerable period of each day measuring *Hydrobia* shells to within 0.2 mm of their total length. This is a menial task, but it has minor compensations, for at the end of the exercise you will know something you did not know before – however trivial the new facts may be. A fellow student designed and built a clanking machine that measured dog-whelks on his behalf, sorting them into size groups and ringing a bell at intervals. He could consequently measure many more shells per hour than I could. But his machine ignored the problem of chipped spines. His task was therefore minimally more boring than mine, for about every five minutes I had to make a decision whether or not to discard a shell, or cheat mildly by entering it in the table and allowing, by means of a good guess, for the broken point. We used to work at a laboratory bench before an immense plate-glass window overlooking Plymouth Sound, with a misty Drake's Island in the middle distance. At frequent intervals we forgot about the length of snail shells and our bickering argument about the damaged whorls, and gazed across the harbour spellbound and lost in thought. In those days I fancied no seascape in the world could hold a candle to Plymouth Sound, with its glittering pathway to the sun, its gorse-capped line of distant cliffs, its infinitely varied sky with bleached sails floating on the horizon, and, nearer the shore and docks, a crazy concourse of craft ranging from massive battleships down to the tiniest spluttering motorboat and tear-away skiff. I don't know how much time we wasted deeply en- grossed in the scene, but it was no doubt quite considerable. Nor do I know what thoughts were passing through my fellow student's mind while he gazed, frowning, at some plume of smoke rising from a boat hidden below the skyline, or compared the sullen clouds of today with the smooth, jade- green and gold sunset of last evening, for we only discussed the rise and fall of snail populations. Later on I switched my attention to the insect world, and flowering meadows replaced the waves of Plymouth Sound. This book is a reflection of the daydreams which, over the years, have consoled

. . . those most improbable tidings

me for the harsh necessity of counting the bristles on the backsides of waistless, wingless fleas.

At this juncture I realised I must find a collaborator – a romantic collaborator to compensate for my own rubber-and-glass mentality. Years spent squeezing the teats of fine pipettes, polishing slides and cover slips, siphoning sea water out of carboys, eliminating bubbles from plankton immersed in oil of cloves, and listening to the monotonous *clink-clunk* of plunger jars concentrates the mind wonderfully, but fails to engender either imagination or a love of poetry.

I found an anonymous collaborator and suddenly the problems were solved. This crazy book – the long-suppressed desire to escape from rubber-and-glass – is about aire and angels. . . . Wings. Doves, the symbol of the spirit, and butterflies, the symbol of the soul.

DIS MANIB. SACR.

C. IVLI SECVLARIS

A dove in one hand and a butterfly in the other

The Soul

You are like my soul a butterfly of dream.[1]

I do not recall who told me I had a soul. Inevitably, during our Bible readings, I must have heard that man had been formed 'of the dust of the ground' and that the Lord God 'breathed into his nostrils the breath of life; and man became a living soul,'[2] but it had made little or no impression upon me. But I do remember that I accepted the fact without question and assumed that the thinking, non-tangible part of me – the part you could not prick with a pin – was my soul, which eventually would be whisked off to heaven when I died.

At the age of eight I read a tale by James Fenimore Cooper. I vividly remember the pale grey binding and elegant title page of that book. It proved difficult to read; there were a great many long words and lengthy descriptions of wild Indian country, and Redskins' habits and the life-style and hardships of the early settlers. I plodded on. Then, suddenly, I came upon an account of two boys returning to their log cabin by the lake after a hunting expedition and finding their grandfather huddled in front of the fire, apparently asleep, with his cap pulled down over his eyes. One of the boys gingerly lifted the cap.

The old man had been scalped.

'My God!' shrieked the boy, frozen with horror.

'There is no God,' mumbled the old man. . . .

I was violently sick.

I continued being sick for 24 hours. At the end of the day I explained tearfully to my mother about the book, about the Red Indians, about the scalping, about God. Then I added: 'You see, I've been thinking . . . and I can't believe there could be room in heaven for all the millions of people who have ever lived and died. . . .'

My mother was one of those rare individuals who describe and comment with penetrating insight, but are rarely if ever lured into argument. On this occasion it was evident that her eight-year-old daughter could not stomach – among other things – the prospect of annihilation, which had dawned on her for the first time. Moreover, it was my mother's belief that children and primitive people need tangible Gods and possibly graven images too, to help and console them for the harsh realities of life.

'You know,' she said authoritatively in a voice which in years to come I affectionately described as Delphic, 'while you were feeling so seedy Lord Haldane came to lunch. He is much, much, *much* cleverer than either you or I, and he believes absolutely in God and an after-life. You see, human minds are not made to *understand* these things, but to *believe* them. We could go crazy trying to count the stars or think of ever-and-ever. You look at the stars and realise that they are uncountable – that the numbers are beyond our imagination. You just accept them – and eternity.'

I don't know to this day whether Haldane's elevation to the status of a graven image, or my mother's calm certainty, or my own ardent desire to have my doubts set at rest achieved the miracle. But I sat up in bed, surreptitiously wiped my nose on a corner of the sheet, accepted the proffered cup of chicken broth, and ceased for ever worrying about my soul and its future cramped living space behind the stars.

This is, in fact a curious characteristic of the soul: by and large it is not a source of concern, worry, and anguish whether people subscribe to sophisticated religions, or the simple, naïve creeds, or no beliefs at all. It is worth remembering that a soul concept has been recorded in every culture known so far to history and ethnography. Edward Wilson suggests that since our deepest feelings are about ourselves, this preoccupation could account for the innermost self – the soul – in mechanistic terms.

I asked my anonymous collaborator whether she believed she had a soul and she evidently did – taking it, I fancy, very much for granted and feeling, like Jung in his student days, that being beyond time and space, it was a suitable candidate for immortality. But not necessarily a subject to dwell on here and now. Nevertheless, when she was a girl, information concerning her soul had given her a consoling sense of freedom, an independence from nightmare ills to which human flesh could well be heir. Bodily she might become paraplegic, but her soul would always be free to wander under the sky.[3]

Why should you weary yourself about a future that is eternal and so cannot be known? asked Horace. True. But then I could not altogether rid myself of anxiety concerning my dog's future life. Poor Nellie was killed by a speeding motor-cycle in Tring High Street. In reply to my anxious query about meeting her again – eventually in heaven, I was told firmly by the stout nursemaid that dogs were soulless animals and did not qualify for paradise. The Iglukik Esquimaux apparently thought otherwise and considered the greatest peril in life lay in the fact that human food consisted entirely of souls, and furthermore the animals struck down and destroyed to make their clothes also had souls, which like their own did not perish

'To fan the moonbeams . . .'

with the body. These resentful, disembodied spirits must be placated. . . . I confess it never occurred to me that my chicken broth or mutton cutlet, let alone my woollen vest had once possessed a soul. I was spared this additional anxiety.

Aristotle, although in no way as confident as the Iglukik Esquimaux, also believed there was an animal soul but was undecided whether or not there were different types of souls for horse, dog, man, or God. Today Richard Swinburne agrees, and believes that animals have a mental life of sensation, thought, purpose, desire, and belief, so they have souls. But there are differences between the mental lives of animals and man, and thus between the capacities of their souls. Aristotle thought we should with reason place the study of the soul in the first rank for 'the soul is the cause and the first principle of the living body'[4] and 'in a sense the soul is all the existing universe.'[5] He also believed that once the white of the egg was complete the animal was being formed and possessed its perceptive

9

soul.* On the other hand, he and the stout nursemaid agreed in one respect, for he said that brutes have only irrational souls; man has in addition a rational soul and only the rational soul is immortal.

The Egyptians taught that after the destruction of the body, the human soul enters into another living being and thus travels through all the animals of the land, the sea, and the birds of the air.

But it was Socrates who first clearly formulated the idea of a non-physical, immaterial soul. This was a revolutionary concept for his contemporaries, who consequently considered him – for this, and perhaps for other reasons too – a perverter of youth. The bewildered Athenians killed him, according to William Ellis thinking mistakenly they would thus be rid of him. His friend Plato, who was also concerned with the problem of personal immortality, provided the core of the Christian doctrines – the philosophy of the immortal psyche and the immaterial God. And Thomas Aquinas was one of those who taught that the human soul keeps its existence when the body breaks up; it was part of Time existing above time, in eternity. But he held that plants and animals had souls and 'all inferior forms as well.' The man in the street who attempts to read up the subject is left even more confused than I was as a child, for he remains wondering uneasily whether he understands what the Greeks and Semites *meant* by psyche or soul. Was it, after all, more than breath of a kind?

It will be recalled that Thomas Hardy's farm-hand knew his companion was dead, not as it appeared just asleep, because he saw a large white moth fly out of his mouth – the man's soul escaping from his body. This event was frequently described in paint by Japanese artists, only their butterfly souls were often multicoloured.

Another crisis developed for me when I was thirteen years old. Strangely enough, although I had played in the farmyard and milked and groomed the cows from the age of seven, I had never realised or understood the reason for castrating the bull calves, nor its consequences. I accepted this treatment as I accepted trimming my toe-nails or cutting half an inch off my pigtail to encourage it to grow. Suddenly this fact of life dawned on me and I was horrified. 'But if a man was castrated,' I asked my mother anxiously, 'wouldn't he fall in love anymore?' Curiously enough I cannot remember her reply but I recall with crystal clarity my profound dismay and the depression that followed. I had very romantic ideas about love. I thought it was something wonderful, concerning the soul and transcending sex and, in fact, had little if anything to do with the act of procreation.

* Today Catholics believe that the soul enters the human foetus at conception but some scientists suggest that gastrulation is the first point at which a body can have a unique soul.

Japanese Butterflies

In order for sexual love to be an experience of true erotic pleasure, suggested Freud – whom I had never heard of – it must be imbued with beauty and express the longings of the soul.

I knew as little about eroticism as I did about Freud, but I was secretly, deeply in love with a captain in the Coldstream Guards – a gentle, reserved soldier three times my age, a friend of the family, who had won the Military Cross at Ypres and filled my head with nebulous, rosy dreams and soulful longings.

In fact I was not a little disturbed by the implications of the castrated bull calves, but on this occasion I did not retire to bed vomiting, but sorrowed silently for lost illusions and blushed at my own embarrassing conclusions. Sadly, I did not know the Kabbalah, which tells us that the Jews had two souls – the 'animal soul,' the vital force, that which keeps men alive and provides the driving force of their lives; and the 'divine soul,' a divine spark which in reality is part of God, deep in the recess of the human psyche.

I would have clutched thankfully at the notion of a divine spark – hidden beneath his immaculate tunic – in the heart of the pale soldier from the Coldstream Guards.

Years and years later I suddenly realised that in many lands and at different times the angelic butterfly was a symbol of the soul. Here was a moment of great delight – at last something even I could understand . . . 'This dull chrysalis cracks into shining wings.'[6]

2

The Spirit

and the Spirit like a dove . . .[1]

'*Soul* includes life, death, divinity, love, meaning, depth and intensity,' wrote Andrew Samuels, 'while spirit is idealistic, exclusive, high-minded.

Soul is about dreams, spirit* about miracles or wishes. It is the difference between *inside* and *outside* . . .'[2]

As a child I accepted the dove as a symbol of the Holy Spirit – or perhaps a bird endowed with the Holy Spirit – without question. As time goes on, one's taste, one's likes and dislikes, enthusiasms, loves, hates, and beliefs are modified or changed, but this particular fervour endured and I still feel today that a white dove is the purest and most perfect expression of life in the natural world.

Before I could read, I received a postcard every day from my mother during her many enforced absences from home. As a subtle form of instruction, she used to send me series illustrating the *chef d'oeuvres* of the great painters and sculptors. I was so deeply moved by El Greco's snowy doves suspended above the Virgin's head in a daze of celestial light that I began to hanker after the Catholic religion – aided and abetted by a proselytizing nanny and a natural passion for gold and silver reflections. But the series came to an end and the postcards switched from Spain to France. I then received a run of glorious Greuze females, draped in blue-and-white satin, with soulful expressions and eyes turned up to heaven. One of them clasped a white pigeon to her breast . . . I was spellbound. After filling two albums with a succession of postcard masterpieces, from primitives to surrealists, what remained for me, clearly and happily, was not the Angel of the Annunciation or Saint Sebastian or Rembrandt or Rosa Bonheur but the Holy Spirit, the white dove.

For there she was in Noah's Ark, and then – after her third sally forth to test the flood waters – she 'returned not again unto him anymore,'[3] preferring her freedom. But she was found again 'in the clefts of the rock, in the secret places of the stairs,'[4] and in the Psalms her wings are 'covered

* Jung suggested spirit was the non-material aspect of man: infinite, spaceless, formless, imageless.

The you-and-I in the street think 'soulless' means insensitivity to non-material factors, and 'spiritless' usually means inert or cowardly. While for many of our acquaintances 'spirit' conjures up a picture of Scotch-on-the-rocks.

The spirit is divisible

Flame of incandescent terror

with silver, and her feathers with yellow gold.'[5] And all four evangelists describe how the heavens opened and the hallowed dove descended and alighted upon Him. And so on and so through the album, until in our time there is Picasso's hesitant little boy, with a white pigeon to blend with his spirit. Fortunately, I did not know that Jewish priests were enjoined to screw off the heads of doves before offering them on the altar to God.

It was years later in the Cathedral at Chartres that a sheet of stained glass brought home to me with some astonishment that the spirit has seven – yes, the magical seven once again – gifts or attributes. We are shown seven doves, representing wisdom, understanding, counsel, fortitude, knowledge, godliness, and the spirit of fear of the Lord.† Curiously enough, in the ancient pre-Christian literature, as well as in even older Chinese literature, we find the dove laying seven eggs. Our doves today stubbornly lay only two.

† The fruits of the Holy Spirit are enumerated in the Douay translation as charity, joy, peace, patience, kindness, goodness, faith, modesty and continency.   (Galatians 5:22-23)

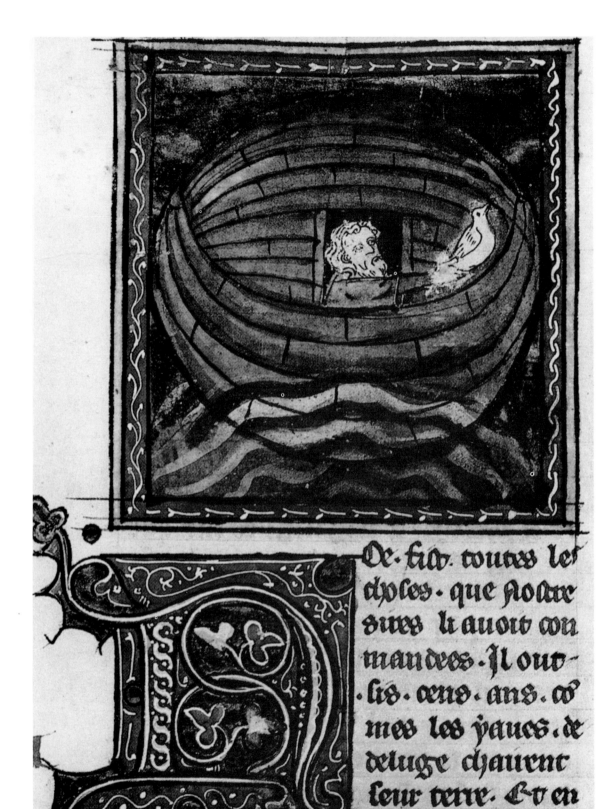

Œe fich toutes les
cposles. que Aolue
sires li auoit con
mandees. Jl oud-
lis. œns. ans. cō
mes les yaues. de
deluge chaurent
leur terre. Et v en
tra. 2 Hoe. et ses

Noah releasing the dove

Simplicity and innocence

Une colombe et moi

Return, oh holy dove, return !

The spirit has varied attributes but the soul is indivisible. Furthermore, the soul embraces the subconscious. But the symbolism down the ages can be a little confusing. On Greek tombstones of young girls in the fourth and fifth centuries B.C., the dove symbolises simplicity and innocence, while in the Roman catacombs it represents human souls rather than the spirit. While even further back in time, described in an Egyptian text of the thirteenth century B.C., the goddess Anath – one of the great goddesses, who conceives but does not bear, who is perennially fruitful but does not lose her virginity – chose the dove as one of her favourite animals, because of its reputed fecundity. A cult stand exists showing a relief of the naked goddess holding two doves in her arms as she sits with her legs apart to display her sex. But Eurynome, the mythical pre-Grecian Goddess of All Things, actually assumed the form of a dove and laid the Universal Egg.

The Roman and Renaissance tombstones, however, show a clear-cut schism between the soul and the spirit, where Cupid and Psyche are placed in juxtaposition. There is one explicit gravestone showing a young lad holding a dove in one hand and a butterfly in the other. But when Saint Benedict's twin sister Saint Scholastica died, he saw her soul take wing as a white dove.

The tomb of a Persian noblewoman, the Empress Nur Jahan, bears a wonderful exhortation:

> Do not decorate my grave with flowers or candles
> Because flowers may deceive the song birds
> And the candle may burn the moth.[6]

Here lies someone who loved butterflies and doves.

I do not know when or how Noah's bird evolved from the carrier of glad tidings into the dove, the 'very blessed spirit of peace,' 'where white investments figure innocence'[7] . . . but Picasso immortalized her thus, although his miraculously earthy pencil turned her into a domestic pigeon of peace. No one has ever understood pigeons as well as Picasso and no one ever will again, but his birds could never symbolise Samuels' Jungian, idealistic, exclusive, high-minded spirit. Peace, perhaps . . .

Not everyone is so definitive as Samuels. Art historian René Huyghe considers the soul something distinct from, and vaster than, the intellect. He tells us the 19th century discovered that the language of the soul was the legitimate domain of Art. But the title of his book is *Art and the Spirit of Man*, and in it he describes art as the language of the human spirit. Huyghe seems to fuse the soul and the spirit, in contrast to the mind, skill and intellect. Freud and Huyghe do not altogether disagree. Freud meant by the

Dove, the love and the spirit

soul (psyche) 'that which is most valuable in man while he is alive.' For him 'the soul is the seat both of the mind and of the passions and we remain largely unconscious of it.'[8]

Psychoanalysis was dedicated to the science of the soul, so much of which remains secret, intangible, inaccessible, deeply hidden . . . but it has nothing to do with immortality or the supernatural, for Freud was a dyed-in-the-wool atheist. His 'soul' may encompass qualities of the spirit but it is far, far removed from the luminous white dove, for whom the heavens split asunder and John bore witness.

3

Love of Things Winged[1]

> Time, as he passes us, has a dove's wing,
> Unsoil'd, and swift, and of a silken sound[2]

It is relatively simple to obtain certain reliable facts about the past and trace the multiple effects of new inventions like the steam engine, or the development of anaesthetics or the camera, but it is much harder to perceive and assess the simultaneous changes that take place in people's daily reactions, moods and feelings. Thus the deep emotions once aroused, for instance, by Victor Hugo's 'Amour des Choses Ailées' are watered down and diminished in an age of aeroplanes and hang-gliders. Gone for ever is the sense of lumpish earth-boundness and feet of clay experienced before we ourselves could fly, and with it has vanished much of the reverence and awe for 'Aire and Angels.'[3] 'Oh that I had wings like a dove!'[4] now sounds rather silly, for if, like the psalmist, we long to escape and 'wander far off,'[5] London airport is within an easy car ride.

> The flying butterfly,
> I feel myself
> A creature of dust.[6]

But the eloquent Japanese poet wrote that verse several centuries before the advent of the shuttle. It is moving, but gently dated.

High up in the mountains above the snowline, or on a lonely shore (out of season!) it is, at times, possible to recapture some of the lost sensations of delight and wonder – watching alpine choughs rise effortlessly into a clear winter sky glittering with stray ice particles, or gulls in a boisterous gale, sailing sideways over a turbulent sea.

> While, poised in air, a bird of snow
> Faltered on lifted wing – to glide
> And glance at this strange to-and-fro . . .[7]

The flight of an insect stirs up a different set of emotions from those engendered by the silver pinions of the dove. Their wings are small and fragile, they are incidental, less remote and less impersonal. The psalmist knew nothing of them. But as a white butterfly flaps past, it arouses in us a sudden sense of recognition, of pleasure and empathy. For somehow they flutter erratically through our lives like stray but familiar thoughts.[8]

Marsh Tern?
STERNA ANGLICA, *Montagu*
Male Summer Plumage

A bird of snow

Imperial Palace Butterflies

> Even the aerobatic swift
> Has not his flying-crooked gift[9]

Both Swinburne and Gautier caught a glimpse of Cabbage Whites flying over the sea – improbable, frangible, almost invisible, like animated snow-flakes for the winds to try.[10] Gautier frankly envied their untracked blue airway.

In Spain a dying man prayed for loving service at his grave so that his liberated soul might linger near. His tombstone bears this inscription: 'Also I therefore command my heirs to entomb my bones, so that the drunken butterfly may flutter over my ashes.'[11] He obviously appreciated haphazard wings.

In China, two thousands years before, a poet wrote:

> Chuang-tzu dreams at sunrise that a butterfly lost its way.
> Wang-ti bequeathed his spring passion to the nightjar.
> The moon is full on the vast sea, a tear on the pearl.
> On Blue Mountain the sun warms, a smoke issues from the jade.[12]

But the Japanese Haiku poets caught the mood of the incidental butterfly better than anyone else before or since. In Haiku there is no desire, no sex, no noise, no war, no laughter, no anger, no urgency – only a detached moment and a faint stab of mild surprise.

> Over the Dianthus
> See. A white butterfly.
> Whose Soul I wonder.[13]

4

Sky-flakes[1]

Lags a turquoise butterfly . . .[2]

Robert Frost puzzled over the irresistible attraction of blue butterflies and tried a little gentle, poetical debunking:

> Why make so much of fragmentary blue
> In here or there a bird, or butterfly,
> Or flower, or wearing-stone, and open eye,
> When heaven presents in sheets the solid hue?[3]

but then he nevertheless wrote:

> It is blue-butterfly day here in spring,
> And with these sky-flakes down in flurry on flurry
> There is more unmixed colour on the wing
> Than flowers will show for days unless they hurry.
>
> But these are flowers that fly and all but sing:
> And now from having ridden out desire
> They lie closed over in the wind and cling
> Where wheels have freshly sliced the April mire.[4]

Kipling also noticed butterflies sitting on the roadway, which is a common event in hotter countries than ours:

> The toad between the harrow knows
> Exactly where each tooth-point goes;
> The butterfly upon the road
> Preaches contentment to that toad.[5]

Some of Elizabeth Barrett Browning's blue butterflies were, I suspect, imaginary, since nature does not seem to have favoured us with the colour scheme she describes in 'Aurora Leigh':

> . . . butterflies, that bear
> Upon their blue wings such red embers round,
> They seem to scorch the blue air into holes[6]

27

Curiously enough, Leconte de Lisle takes almost the same poetic licence and his butterflies have azure-tinted and scarlet wings,[7] but they lack the red circles. Milton was more restrained, for his creatures 'waved their limber fans' but they were invested only with *spots* of gold, purple, green, and azure.[8]

Keats liked the smallness of our blue butterflies . . .

> . . . little bright-eyed things
> That float about the air on azure wings[9]

Browning too, liked the 'tinier blue.'[10]

Neruda, with the sure touch of twentieth-century romance, sends his true love a letter (recorded delivery) enclosing

> A single iris
> And three blue butterfly's wings.[11]

In the tropics these astonishing insects have a totally different character from *our* casual fragments of the sky, quietly opening and shutting their wings among the yellow vetches on the chalk downland. They are large, powerful, sweeping flyers of improbable brilliance, like bright triangles of metallic material sprayed forth by some hidden volcano.

In the Upanishads the greatest hymn of praise was expressed thus:

> Thou art the deep blue butterfly
> Thou art the parrot, green with red eyes,
> Thou art the father of lightning.
> Thou art the seasons and the seas.[12]

From the entomologist's point of view, blue is the most fascinating of all the wing colours. Two principal systems are involved in producing these fabulous effects: the chemistry of pigments – selective absorption – and the physics of thin-film interference. The pigments, many of which are plant-derived, are usually contained within the scale vestiture that covers the insect's wings. It can easily be brushed off, and this produces the fine dust beloved of poets. Heine in a playful and charming love poem saw butterflies 'teasingly scatter their coloured diamond dust in the flowers' eyes.'[13] The French poet de Vigny also wrote of his butterflies passing on powdery wings,[14] and a Chinese poet, in a different mood, describes how

> The light on the pool suddenly hides the wall,
> Mingled scents of flowers invade the room,
> On the edge of the screen, powder smeared by the butterfly:
> On the lacquered window the yellow print of the bee.[15]

But the mealy wings are the most felicitous.

LEPIDOPTERA.

Papilio Menelaus, var.　　　*Papilio Rhetenor*, cram.

London Published as the Act directs by E.Donovan, March 1. 1798.

Thou art the deep blue butterfly . . .

Although blue colouration is almost always found within the scales, this is not necessarily so; an electric blue and black Swallowtail has its wing membranes loaded with blue pigments (pterobilins) which can be seen from without, because the scales that would normally hide them from view are modified and reduced to mere threads. The function of these particular bile pigments – only found in butterflies and moths – is not clearly understood, but with the aid of an electron microscope one can see that in the blue region of the membranes they are studded with hundreds of lens-like protuberances. Do they focus light rays from without or reflect them from within? We do not know.

The flashing iridescent metallic blue of the butterflies of the South American forest and scrublands is produced by the micro-structure of the scales. Light rays are refracted and diffused as they fall on the thin, thin, microscopic ridges and grooves, thus producing the paradisial interference phenomenon.

It is not surprising to find that in the past, as we have seen, many groups of people in Central and South America worshipped butterflies. Flowers, butterflies, and water were sacred symbols of the Nahuas and the Mayas. Butterflies were venerated by the ancient Mexicans and at times worshipped as their god of love and beauty and as a patron of domestic work. Butterfly eggs were called *ahuauhpapalotl* – seeds of happiness.

> I? who am I?
> I live as a fugitive, singer of flowers.
> Songs I make
> and butterflies of song.
> They bloom in my soul
> so that my heart may taste them.[16]

Butterflies were also associated with the symbols of heat, light and regeneration, and the Goddess of earth and the stars. Itzpapalote, the Obsidian butterfly, was named after hard, black, shiny volcanic glass.

> The Goddess is upon the rounded cactus:
> she is our Mother, Obsidian Butterfly.
> O, let us look upon Her.
> She is fed upon stags' hearts in the Nine Plains.
> She is our Mother, Queen of the Earth.[17]

Curiously enough, in the pre-Columbian world, butterflies were often connected with war and violence and human sacrifice. Xochiquetzal, companion of the fire god, followed young warriors onto the battlefield and had intercourse with them, holding a butterfly between her lips.

Blue Butterfly Day

The ancient Mexicans regarded one of the large nocturnal moths with fear akin to horror – miquipapalotl, butterfly of death.[18] It was easily attracted to natural light and its appearance in a room at night was considered an ill omen – butterfly of dread and terror, the frightful butterfly or the sacred butterfly.

Eventually when the god-king Quetzalcóatl abolished human sacrifice, butterflies were burnt alive as a sacred replacement.

5

Roses and Butterflies

Even the butterfly rests on the rose[1]

Poets and sculptors, great and small, link roses and butterflies. Even engraved stones at the time of the Roman emperors showed a butterfly hovering over a rose.

Keats wrote:

> A butterfly, with golden wings broad parted
> Nestling a rose, convulsed as though it smarted
> With over-pleasure[2]

Yeats suggested that butterflies ate roses, but he did not indicate at what stage of their life cycle:

> This great purple butterfly,
> In the prison of my hands,
> Has a learning in his eye
> Not a poor fool understands.
>
> Once he lived a schoolmaster
> With a stark, denying look;
> A string of scholars went in fear
> Of his great birch and his great book.
>
> Like the clangour of a bell,
> Sweet and harsh, harsh and sweet,
> That is how he learnt so well
> To take the roses for his meat.[3]

The German poet Heine remarked: With the rose the butterfly is deeply in love.[4] And Sainte-Beuve's butterfly is drawn to the rose it has kissed.[5]

The lesser fry follow suit:

> The chaste butterfly
> The bumbling bumble bee
> Do they not love the chalice of the rose?[6]

Even the butterfly rests on the rose

Born with the spring, dying with the rose . . .

and again:

> Let me smell the wild white rose . . .
> Sated from their blossoms rise
> Honey bee and butterflies[7]

The two were linked in a French poem with a marvellous first line which, alas, loses everything in translation:

> *Naître avec le printemps, mourir avec les roses . . .*[*][8]

Lamartine goes on to compare the butterfly and desire:

> *Sur l'aile du zéphyr nager dans un ciel pur ;*
> *Balancé sur le sein des fleurs à peine écloses.*
> *S'enivrer de parfums, de lumière et d'azur ;*
> *Secouant, jeune encore, la poudre de ses ailes,*
> *S'envoler comme un souffle aux voûtes éternelles,*
> *Voilà du papillon le destin enchanté.*
> *Il ressemble au désir, qui jamais ne se pose,*
> *Et, sans se satisfaire, effleurant toute chose,*
> *Retourne enfin au ciel chercher la volupté !*

Virginia Woolf really understood the Lepidoptera but in a letter to Vita Sackville-West she was dubious about this relationship.

> 'It's all very well about . . . Persia being a rose and you an Emperor moth . . .'[9]

In *Swann's Way* they are linked with roses and zephyrs:

> . . . Come with the glorious silken raiment of the lily, apparel fit for Solomon, and with the many-coloured enamel of the pansies, but come, above all, with the spring breeze, still cooled by the last frosts of winter, wafting apart, for the two butterflies' sake, that have waited outside all morning, the closed portals of the first Jerusalem rose.[10]

Even that superlative and uncanny observer Marcel Proust was wondering in error, for all this is pure poet's fancy or licence, for roses do not attract moths or butterflies. Neither their scent, nor their nectar, nor their pollen appeals to them. They pass by indifferently on mealy wings.[11] Roses are beetle flowers, evolved and specialised to allure the iridescent chafers and Longicorns, not careless butterflies.[12]

---

* Born with the spring, dying with the rose.

6

Clothes Moths

The Bible, which ignores butterflies, presents us with two very attractive comments on clothes moths. In the Psalms we are told:

> Thou makest his beauty to consume away like as it were a moth fretting a garment[1]

and Matthew warns us:

> Lay not up for yourselves treasures upon earth where moth and rust doth corrupt . . .[2]

Tolstoy also ignores butterflies but he gives us a nice description of the lawyer advising Karenin on his contemplated divorce and surreptitiously catching clothes moths which fly past his desk.

> The lawyer, with a rapidity one could not have expected of him, opened his hands, caught the moth, and resumed his former attitude. By the end of the interview he felt so cheerful that contrary to his custom he let the haggling lady have a reduction and stopped catching moths, having finally decided to have his furniture re-upholstered next winter in plush . . .[3]

Today, unlike sixty years ago, clothes moths which, as caterpillars, eat domestic materials rather than plants, are relatively rare in my house – chemical warfare has triumphed.

But the poets are attracted by this little insect's colourless anonymity and its quick flash of self-effacing activity.

> . . . in the hazardous light
> of earth's familiar moon;
> A clothes-moth winged from left to right . . .[4]

Shelley, in his *Defence of Poetry*, tells us that . . . epitomes have been called the moths of just history; they eat out the poetry of it.[5]

7

The Garden and Your Room

Blue passion flower!
Like an anvil battered by butterflies . . .[1]

There are certain scenes – like certain expressions on people's faces – which become part of your life, and when you suddenly catch sight of them you relive the past and experience once again the emotions you had – strangely enough – quite forgotten. One such moment occurred when I discovered the great beauty of flowering branches of Norway Maple – leafless of course at this period – seen against a white wall. It was the first week of March and I could not resist an act of mild vandalism when I came across a fairly young tree on the edge of the wood, alight with a mass of bright green flowers – spreading panicles at the end of bare branches. The flowers seemed to incorporate the pale March sunlight and threw fragile shadows against the white wall. Through the window you could see thrusts of snowdrops among dry brown leaves.

This episode altered my approach to flowers in the home. Up to that time they had been, for me, still-life pictures, and I arranged them like a misty Odilon Redon bouquet, or a rush of stark Dufy arums, or a vase of iris kept until they faded into Anna Ticho's tender, poetic vision of overness. Inevitably there was a period when I became hooked on Dutch still-life.

I began to grow old-fashioned Rembrandt tulips – three main varieties, striped pink and white, yellow and brown, black and cream – to serve as a central theme for Dutch arrangements. A bowl of ripe cherries or a bunch of grapes – they had to be fresh, with the bloom much in evidence – were placed alongside. I felt these pictures were painted by artists who really loved gardening and sunshine and expressed their love with bewitching realism. The plethora of insects that embellished their garlands of flowers was astonishing and delightful. Much later I was introduced to the *vanitas* theme and the symbolism of Dutch still-life painting – the empty glass lying on its side, miraculously transparent, the skull, the roll of parchment and the ephemeral butterfly had to take on a new and faintly melancholy significance. A professor of Art History suggests that the ubiquitous white butterfly – for it appears on almost every painting – is equated with virtue, resurrection, and immortality, while the Red Admiral, black and scarlet, symbolises death or damnation. But surely the magpie moths and red and striped tigers, which adorn so many bouquets, are included because of their colours and improbable patterns. For the enlightenment of my small son who was at that time a keen collector, I ran a moth trap in the garden. The hawkmoths and tigers, so much in evidence in the Dutch pictures, were removed sound asleep at daybreak and introduced to the flowers in the central vase on the dining-room table. After shuffling their feet they settled down to doze away the hours of daylight – exquisite ornaments which amazed those visitors who noticed them; some never did. On one occasion a learned professor leaned across the table and addressed my son, who was silently eating his lunch. 'Boy!' he said in a rather severe tone. 'Boy! I fear you have an insect in your hair.' 'I know,' said Charles politely – who by this time was familiar with all the species that filtered into the trap, and who had a special affection for the Noctuids – 'It's my Frosted Orange. It matches my hair, sort of. . . .'

My addiction to the Dutch masters was intense but transient; it brought home to me forcibly the fact that very few painters consider the flowers as part of the room.

The focus is on the blooms themselves. Even when the underlying theme is the brevity of man's life on earth, or his thirst for knowledge, or his insatiable greed, they never go beyond the table, an overturned goblet, and a white butterfly. These remarks do not only apply to the Dutch masters. It is true also if the artist is drawing fritillaries – a purple flower 'chequered with white'[2] on vellum for a botanical treatise, or roses and lilies are rioting forth from an elaborate marble cornucopia, or a floral design wreathing the Virgin Mary. But the Norway maple changed all this for me. I stopped thinking of a parsimonious Japanese brush drawing or Rembrandt tulips adorned with gilded butterflies. From then onwards I arranged flowers for the room and its link with the garden beyond the window. Especially the open window.

If you can't paint – which is very frustrating for a gardener – you have to create your own pictures, and fortunately the seasons see to it that you have a chance to view them again next year.

My sitting-room widows are divided from the outside world by fine metal curtains, with links about six inches apart, and I found that they provided an ideal and most unobtrusive trellis for Ipomoea, 'Heavenly Blue.' From a fair-sized earthenware pot in the corner of the window-sill the plants romp up the sides of the curtains and soon smother them with their brilliant cerulean flowers.

Symbol of virtue, resurrection and immortality

The Red Admiral *symbolises Death or Damnation*

Blue, silver white and budded Tyrian![3]

The great attraction of this arrangement is that both the flowers and their leaves are seen against the light – the windows face south – so that before noon the room is filled with a shadowy blue and emerald essence. I make a point of growing pale mauve Clematis (several species, some early and some late) up the outside wall of the house and alongside the windows. I have described elsewhere my weakness for a juxtaposition of blue and mauve flowers. So that on the lawn below the window there is a mixture of purple crocus and early *Chionodoxa*, and later the two colours are linked by the fringe of cornflowers and mauve corncockle along the edge of the gravel path. I once tried growing 'Nellie Moser' up the metal curtains, mixed with the *Ipomoea*, but the room began to look vaguely like a conservatory

Roses and daffodils rioting forth

Butterfly screen

– which is something I avoid at all costs. I would not mind *living* in a hot-house with tropical plants, but I do not want to confuse it with the room in which I write and very occasionally *think*. Nor must it resemble the expensive pot-planted, luxurious offices that now characterize big business in the United States. As a wild climber in its native land, there is nothing more beautiful than the fragrant, waxy white flowers and leathery green leaves of *Stephanotis*, but I confess its relentless appearance as a backcloth to the word processor and the screen printer has extinguished some of its magic and mystery.

I am passionately fond of roses and *if* I have a favourite flower at this moment in midwinter, it is the Dog-rose, which is a blissfully untidy plant. Roses are the flowers par excellence for the library. I see to it that various old-fashioned varieties like William Allen Richardson and Golden Dawn scramble all over the outside of the house and blur the outline of every window frame, but there is something profoundly moving about a bowl of full-blown roses against a background of books ranged on tall shelves – especially the drooping lemon-yellow ones like Maréchal Niel, which enhances every binding, from brown leather tooled in gold to a conglomeration of battered French paperbacks.

In the kitchen garden, flanked by blackberries growing on wire frames and nectarines trained along a wall, I have planted a 100-yard strip of roses, two deep, which are grown purely for use as cut flowers – with a thought for the books as the ultimate backcloth. For one all too brief period in midsummer I can fill a bowl with 'Étoile d'Hollande,' adding a few Admiral Rodney to *épater les bourgeois* – then suddenly the atmosphere of the library changes, the shelves recede, and attention is focused on the table and one of the great creative triumphs of man – the most beautifully shaped, coloured, and scented flower in the world and the great love of every rightminded beetle.

Once in a while during the summer – rather late in the day – 'Sterling Silver' and 'Blue Moon' decide, after all, to produce a few flowers. The scent of these roses is indescribably sweet and melancholy. They are destined for a cut-glass vase on the library mantelpiece, set against the pale limed oak panelling. I find 'Blue Moon' unreasonably, irritatingly sparse with her flowers – a nervous rose whose smoky reticence makes her the ideal companion for the thin erudite books of reference that flank the fireplace.

My family are resigned to the fact that, as time passes, I become less and less attracted by conventional gardening and the fields edge nearer and nearer to the house itself. One of the links is the wild roses that grow along the terrace walls and even mingle with the cultivated varieties climbing about the house itself. Guests, on driving into the courtyard, look at the tangle of unkempt plants and wonder uneasily if they have come to the right address. Can anyone really *live* here? I have discovered that a great many plants reaching for the light will scale the walls. Good old *Buddleia davidii* waves its flowers over the first-floor balcony 15 feet from the ground. And Red Admirals, Painted Ladies, Meadow Browns, and Hairstreaks flit round the open bedroom windows. Occasionally a small Tortoiseshell finds its way inside:

> And there will fly into the room
> A coloured butterfly in silk
> To flutter, rustle and pitter pat
> On the blue ceiling[4]

Sweet peas, broom, ivy, roses, clematis, Virginia creeper, old man's beard, cherry, Japanese quince, wisteria, laburnum, and lilac compete for wall space. Lavender is planted beneath the ground-floor windows and we are rewarded by a snowstorm of white butterflies – insects that taste with their feet as well as their tongues – crowding onto these flowers.

For better or for worse you spend quite a large slice of your time in the kitchen. This room is also protected with a thin metal curtain. Here the scarlet runner bean takes the place of *Ipomoea* and whisks towards the ceiling like a firework. This plant, when first introduced to the United Kingdom, came as a decorative flower, not a vegetable, but in this role it has been sadly neglected. In the kitchen all depends on the receptacle you choose for your flowers. Gentians stuffed into one of those black-brown teapots are electrifying, and willow catkins in a copper kettle in the window bring April along with the scones and fresh cream.

As the fields edge forward, I have become a bulb-and-grass gardener. I think all I want is a flowering hayfield rich in *Fritillaria*, merging into a medieval Botticelli or pre-Raphaelite covered lawn, with all the starry, low-growing flowers, from dim violets to buttercups and daisies. The wave must stop at the foot of the stonework and lead, with a riot of climbing roses, to the sophisticated hot- and cold-house plants looking out of the window. I almost achieve this towards the end of the summer. For then I grow the arable weeds along the narrow strip of no-man's land between the grass and gravel path. They can't compete with the flora of a hayfield, but here I can promote a border of poppies, perennial flax, cornflowers, corn marigold, and corncockle and some of the less aggressive grasses. Old man's beard festoons the dining-room window, framing the *Gloriosa* within.

I have a few plants of the original *G. rothschildii*, which has a much tougher petal with a stouter, crinkly yellow edge than the variety (or species?) called by that name that is sold on the market today. It is a wonderfully easy flower to arrange in a vase, for the plant is so subtly photopositive that the flowers all shift themselves to the outside of the bouquet, like candles placed on a Christmas tree. It is one of those lilies that open backwards: the petals first come to lie flat, and then lash towards the rear like the ears of a vicious horse. The way flowers open never ceases to surprise me; most astonishing of all are the flannel flowers (*Hoya*), which snap open from a central point – a whorl of clockwork toys – while the yellow Oxalis is rolled up neatly like a folded umbrella. I marvel too at the petals of the field poppies, which instead of being carefully layered inside the calyx are crushed together – a bundle of crumpled red rags which don't unfold but are shaken out. . . . They never quite lose their creases.

We should be deeply grateful to Claude Monet for immortalizing that field of poppies (and the parasol!) – flowers that are now being bulldozed and weed-killered out of our lives. For that reason if for no other, we need them now along the gravel path. At times who can resist grabbing a white enamel bucket and sneaking Monet's field into the sitting room, poppies and wild barley predominating? And then you keep adding. First the cockle, then quaking grass, and Yorkshire fog, then one cornflower and another. Then you put the bucket in the empty fireplace. . . . Once in a while a Silver-Y moth whizzes in through the open terrace door and unerringly finds the bucket, as if drawn by an invisible magnet.

The contrast between the cornfields' idle weeds and the hayfield flowers, which are miniscule stars in a green firmament, ebbing towards the stone walls, and the carefully and skilfully grown velvety rose and silver lily – taking over the room, books and all – engenders a strange emotion. Vague, evocative, slightly melancholy – something you hanker after, without really knowing why. But strangely enough, almost perversely, the most beautiful picture I have ever seen successfully linking the garden and the house is Bonnard's *Open Window*. You look out of this shady room to the hushed timelessness of the blazing summer sunlight. High noon. There are no flowers in the garden. Trees . . . The vastest breathers of the air.

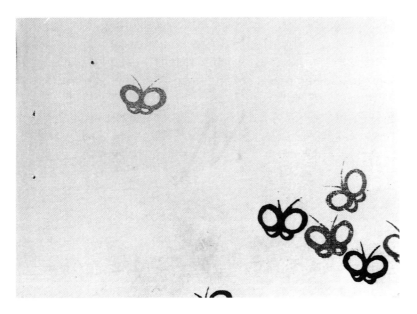

You are the butterfly and I the dreaming heart

8

Candles

> Some there be that shadows kiss;
> Such hath but a shadow's bliss . . .
> Thus hath the candle singed the moth.[1]

A lovely picture of the moth/candle theme was painted by Balthus and titled *La Phalène* (The Moth). Only he elected to paint an oil lamp with a glass chimney, not the classical candle. Balthus and Nabokov were gifted interpreters and fellow lovers of nymphets – provocative, awkwardly natural, deliciously untidy, difficult and infinitely desirable, but still – as far as we are concerned – living in an alien, schoolroom world. Balthus' moth-nymphet is stark naked and about to go to bed. A stocking – or possibly a face towel, for Balthus was fascinated by little girls' ablutions – is hanging from her left hand; the other is reaching out for the fluttering insect, both rendered luminous, transparent and unearthly in the light of the lamp. Quietly crawling up the bedclothes – ignored by the title – is a second, less ethereal, dull brown moth, bemused by the glare. The dream and the reality.

One of the forgotten pleasures of life is candlelight. No matter how subtly our bulbs are shaded, concealed, camouflaged, decorated, or transformed it is impossible, with electricity, to recapture the quiet, flattering, and enchanting light of wax candles and their incandescent haloes. A moth banging against an electric bulb in your bedroom or rattling around in the protective metal cover of a street arc-lamp engenders a sense of irritation only, tinged with concern. It has no romance or anguish.

> Has no-one . . . warned you how despairing
> The moths are when they are burned?[2]

and in *Green Mansions*:

A moth that perished in the flame; an indistinct faint sound; a dream in the night.[3]

and again:

> That's a handsome moth
> Come in to die, two petals, two tendrils
> And a flake of snow, meticulous, irrelevant,
> Unwise.[4]

You sense the difference.

'Some there be that shadows kiss'

And the butterflies began to sing

The scientists don't really know why moths are irresistibly attracted to light, and they remark lamely that the insect's response 'suggests that it has some biological meaning for these animals.' But at least they now know that moths migrating at night can navigate by the moon and, if there is no moon, by the stars. Pliny had some very curious and obscure reflections on the subject:

> The moth that is seen fluttering about the flame of a lamp is generally reckoned in the number of noxious medicaments;* its bad effects are neutralized by the agency of goat's liver.[5]

*Pliny considered that moths' wings usually provided curative medicaments, although their bodies were deadly.

48

Walter de la Mare was the great poet of little things, and his moth stares from glamorous eyes, wafted on plumes like mist.

> Isled in the midnight air
> Musked with the dark's faint bloom,
> Out into glooming and secret haunts
> The flame cries 'Come!'[6]

The poets' intuition failed them where the nectar of roses was concerned, but they have been right in linking moths and celestial cues. The imperious nature of the light lure, which leads them to perish in our civilized habitat, impressed Don Marquis:

> i was talking to a moth
> the other evening
> he was trying to break into
> an electric light bulb
> and fry himself in the wires
>
> 'it is better to be happy
> for a moment
> and be burned up with beauty
> than to live for a long time . . .'
>
> i do not agree with him
> but at the same time i wish
> there was something i wanted
> as badly as he wanted to fry himself[7]

And Shelley, with his sixth sense, knew 'the desire of the moth for the star.'[8]

Boswell, as usual, successfully relates everything to his relationship with Johnson:

I teized him with fanciful apprehensions of unhappiness. A moth having fluttered round the candle, and burnt itself, he laid hold of this little incident to admonish me; saying with a sly look, and in a solemn but quiet tone, 'That creature was its own tormentor, and I believe its name was BOSWELL.'[9]

Thomas Hardy is the master of the rural scene – the reality of country life rather than the dreams of poets. Diggory Venn and Wildeve were playing at dice on the heath at night by the light of a lantern.

The flame cries 'Come!'

Ten minutes passed away. Then a large death's head moth advanced from the obscure outer air, wheeled twice round the lantern, flew straight at the candle and extinguished it by the force of the blow. Wildeve had just thrown, but not lifted the box to see what he had cast; and now it was impossible.[10]

The lantern theme is repeated in Góngora's *Second Solitude*:

> . . . and at last a crystal butterfly,
> – not winged, but waved –
> expires at Tetis' lantern by the shore.[11]

and sometimes an electric lamp takes its place:

The air was velvety and warm, around a milky white arc light swirled pale midges and one ample dark moth with hoary margins.[12]

Nabokov caught the desolation of the deserted railway station:

Like moons round Jupiter, pale moths revolved about a lone lamp. A dismembered newspaper stirred on a bench. Somewhere on the train one could hear muffled voices. . . .[13]

And again:

A little later the train began to move, but then stopped for good, emitting a long, softly sibilant sigh of relief, and simultaneously pale stripes of light passed slowly across the dark compartment . . . Several midges and one large moth circled around a gas lantern; shadowy people shuffled along the platform conversing about unknown things as they went; then there was a jangle of buffers and the train glided off.[14]

And still steeped in gloom:

> Under the smiling lamp
> A mass of life lies down to die.
> Moths, sample snippets of a finished stamp[15]

In Renaissance Emblem Books the moth/candle theme figures as a love emblem. Donne wrote:

> Thy heart seem'd waxe, and steele thy constancy
> . . . so, the taper's beamie eye
> Amorously twinkling, beckons the giddie flie,
> Yet burns his wings.[16]

And Eliot wrote of Donne and love – but not of butterflies and candles:

> Donne, I suppose, was such another
> Who found no substitute for sense,
> To seize, to clutch, to penetrate
> Expert beyond experience,
>
> He knew the anguish of the marrow
> The ague of the skeleton;
> No contact possible to flesh
> Allayed the fever of the bone.[17]

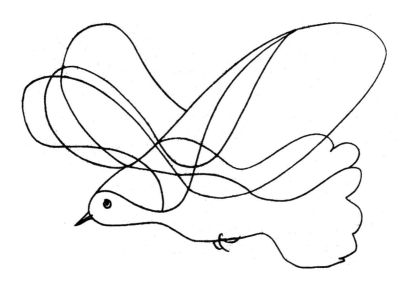

9

Vladimir Nabokov and the Small Gilded Fly[1]

Literature and butterflies are the two sweetest passions known to man.[2]

We are told that several thousand years ago in Mexico groups of people worshipped butterflies; it was not only the ancient Greeks and Japanese who believed they were souls of the departed. Judging by the grace and fidelity with which the ancient Egyptian scribes delineated *Danaus chrysippus egyptius*, they too understood and enjoyed these delightful creatures. Even the illuminated manuscripts of the Dark Ages reveal that the monks numbered among them some excellent entomologists. I was surprised to find a Meadow Brown with a familiar spot count sitting amid the gilded capitals of a Book of Hours in a sumptuous museum in New York City.

Thomas Browne was awestruck by the metamorphosis of butterflies:

> Those strange and mystical transmigrations that I have observed in Silkewormes, turn'd my Philosophy into Divinity. There is in these works of Nature, which seeme to puzzle reason, something Divine, and hath more in it than the eye of a common spectator doth discover.[3]

Perhaps the explanation of the sale of 100,000 copies of Riley and Higgins' book on the butterflies of Europe lies not in the highly commendable mushrooming of interest in the fauna of the EEC, but in the remnant of butterfly worship that lingers within us all.

Possibly the most attractive contribution English writers have made to contemporary literature is their interpretation and uncanny understanding of leisure. Siegfried Sassoon was the most evocative leaner-over-gates the world has ever known. In *The Old Century and Seven More Years* he describes how one morning, gazing into the distance from his airy attic window, his agreeable reverie was disturbed by the fluttering of a butterfly imprisoned between the skylight and the gauze tacked over it to soften the glare:

> By standing on a chair – which I placed on a table – I could just get my hand between the gauze and the glass. The butterfly was ungratefully elusive and more than once the chair almost toppled over. Successful at last I climbed down and was about to put the butterfly out of the window when I observed between my fingers that it wasn't the Small Tortoiseshell that I had assumed it to be. Its dark wings had yellowish borders with blue spots on them. It was more than seven years since

Fowling in the Marshes

I had entomologically squeezed the thorax of a 'specimen.' Doing so now I discovered that one of the loftiest ambitions of my childhood had belatedly been realised – I had caught a Camberwell Beauty.[4]

Dr. Zhivago, on the other hand, had no nostalgic memories of hot summer afternoons in short pants, but like Shakespeare and Dante he nonetheless had a feeling for butterflies. He popped them in a corner of one of his giant canvases of revolution, love, and timeless Russian landscapes, just as Dürer placed his stag beetle at the feet of the Virgin Mary. In so doing he provided us with a marvellous vignette of a cryptic Satyrid going to rest:

It is after your sweat . . .

Folding and unfolding like a scrap of coloured material a brown speckled butterfly flew across the sunny side of the clearing. Yuri watched it sleepily. Choosing a background colour nearest to its own it settled on the brown speckled bark of a pine tree and disappeared into it.[5]

Browning occasionally had moments of a naturalist's insight, mixed with poetry, and noted that butterflies squabbled at nectar sources:

> For the prize were great butterflies fighting,
> Some five for one cup. . . .[6]

French poets, on the other hand, experience a purely emotional reaction, and their golden butterflies are for ever gliding across sunlit scented meadows – stemless blossoms.

The lepidopterists themselves, one records with regret, have made no notable contributions to literature. We lack an Izaak Walton, and even Gilbert White did not really appreciate insects. There have been some splendid and eloquent morphological descriptions by Lord Rothschild, for example, who had an insatiably possessive love for the whole group (two and a half million set specimens), but he, like many others, smashed his butterflies on the systematist's wheel. Vladimir Nabokov, however, was the miraculous exception – the Russian man of letters and professional entomologist rolled into one; the ardent butterfly collector, the evocative wizard of words, the creator of Lolita, the author of *Lysandra cormion*, and the captor of Nabokov's Pug – the man who could at last describe with understanding and poetic eloquence the unspoken emotions of ten thousand inhibited and pen-tied lepidopterists.

Listen to Nabokov:

On the other side of the river, a dense crowd of small, bright blue male butterflies that had been tippling on the rich, trampled mud and cow dung through which I trudged rose all together into the spangled air and settled again as soon as I had passed.

After making my way through some pine groves and alder scrub I came to the bog. No sooner had my ear caught the hum of diptera around me, the guttural cry of a snipe overhead, the gulping sound of the morass under my foot, than I knew I would find here quite special arctic butterflies, whose pictures, or, still better nonillustrated descriptions I had worshipped for several seasons. And the next moment I was among them. Over the small shrubs of bog bilberry with fruit of a dim, dreamy blue, over the brown eye of stagnant water, over moss

'. . . a brown speckled butterfly flew across the sunny side of the clearing'.

and mire, over the flower spikes of the fragrant bog orchid (the *nochnaya fialka* of Russian poets), a dusky little Fritillary bearing the name of a Norse goddess passed in a low skimming flight. Pretty Cordigera, a gemlike moth, buzzed all over its uliginose food plant. I pursued rose-margined Sulphurs, gray-marbled Satyrs. Unmindful of the mosquitoes that furred my forearms, I stooped with a grunt of delight to snuff out the life of some silver-studded lepidopteron throbbing in the folds of my net. Through the smells of the bog, I caught the subtle perfume of butterfly wings on my fingers, a perfume which varies with the species – vanilla, or lemon, or musk, or a musty, sweetish odour difficult to define. Still unsated, I pressed forward. At last I saw I had come to the end of the marsh. The rising ground beyond was a paradise of lupines, columbines, and pentstemons. Mariposa lilies bloomed under Ponderosa pines . . .[7]

Nabokov's greatest gift was not the presentation of the Purple Emperor in our dream net, but the miraculous capture of that elusive period of child-hood which *imprints* the countryside with its scents and sounds and sunlight and shadows in our bones rather than our minds. He describes this feeling of union with delight and felicity:

And the highest enjoyment of timelessness – in a landscape selected at random – is when I stand among rare butterflies and their food plants. This is ecstasy, and behind the ecstasy is something else, which is hard to explain. It is like a momentary vacuum into which rushes all that I love. A sense of oneness with sun and stone. A thrill of gratitude to whom it may concern – to the contrapuntal genius of human fate or to tender ghosts humoring a lucky mortal.[8]

Theoretically, Nabokov should not have been a good systematist – for once he had left the schoolroom, his love for the 'leps' was probably more aesthetic than scientific – but his revision of the neotropical blues (*Psyche*, 1945) was excellent and his descriptions of the dozen new species and sub-species he described were neat, competent, accurate, and useful. Although his output was small it was impeccable, supported by an impressive background of general information. He spent six years in the Harvard Museum of Comparative Zoology as a Research Fellow in Entomology and added several thousand specimens to their collection and that of the American Museum of Natural History.

Nabokov possessed a sardonic brand of entomological humour. He once found a Lycaenid pinned on a cork with a 'new species?' query alongside. When the owner of the specimen returned to his desk he found a neat label in Nabokov's handwriting attached to the butterfly inscribed '*Thecla caramba* Hewitson.' This involved him in the awful task of comparing the scores of Hewitson types – only to find, at the end of his search, that no such species existed. Later a friend pointed out that *caramba* in Spanish could signify 'damn' or 'hell' or 'what a shame!' He decided to use the name, which seemed remarkably appropriate.

Fundamentally, Nabokov enjoyed the excitement of entomological exploration and felt it had provided him with some of the greatest thrills of his life. It was a slender and tensile thread linking all the rather disconnected periods together. After a happy childhood in a united, well-to-do household in Russia, he survived a revolution and his beloved father's assassination; he also experienced the dreary, traumatic business of the impecunious refugee, teaching languages in Berlin, London and Paris, and the blaze of fame and fortune that attended the projection onto paper of the chase after the human version of the Lycaenids; not forgetting the academic period in Boston and the dubious Hollywood experience, we find Nabokov in middle age catching hawkmoths round a strip of neon lighting in Texas, and again as a fat, hatless old man in shorts, collecting assiduously in the alpine meadows above Montreux.

He truly loved the angelic butterfly.

10

Silk

The worms were hallow'd that did breed the silk[1]

Silk is the most beautiful material in the world. Poets cherished it.

> Whereas in silks my Julia goes,
> Then, then, (methinks) how sweetly flows
> That liquefaction of her clothes.
>
> Next, when I cast mine eyes and see
> That brave Vibration each way free;
> – O how that glittering taketh me![2]

and again:

> Look down stars, you illimitable wakers,
> On her delight that wakes from silks[3]

The Chinese empress Si Ling-chi bestowed her royal favour on the industry twenty-six hundred years before Christ, and thereafter the export of live material from China was made punishable by death. It was a secret jealously guarded for the next three thousand years. Nevertheless the economic potential of silk was so great that it was inevitable that, sooner or later, some ingenious method for its export would be devised. Legend has it that a Chinese princess who had married a Bucharan prince in the fourth century arrived for her nuptials with the eggs of the silk moth concealed in her hair. The offspring of those insects, some hundred years later, were distributed to Rome, and the European silk commerce was born. The woven fabric, however, was so expensive in Roman times that even nobles could not afford garments made of whole silk (*holosirikon*) and had to be content with a mixture of half silk and wool or linen (*semisirikon*)[4].* Chaucer tells us that the Maunciple's spoilt cat made his 'couch of silk.'[5]

---

* These dresses were so fine [wrote Pliny] as to be transparent and were sometimes dyed purple and enriched with stripes of gold. . . . "Nor, in fact, have the men even felt ashamed to make use of garments formed of this material in consequence of their extreme lightness in summer: for so greatly have manners degenerated in our day that, so far from wearing a cuirass, a garment even is found to be too heavy".[4]

A symbol of immortality, abundant leisure and joy

The material is only rarely mentioned in the Bible, but in Ezekiel, where God describes his love for Jerusalem, He says:

> Behold thy time was the time of love . . . I clothed thee also with broidered work, and shod thee with badgers' skin, and I girded thee about with fine linen, and I covered thee with silk.[6]

and it will be remembered that the virtuous woman was clothed in 'silk and purple.'[7]

Curiously enough, its use for making the wicks of Sabbath lamps was forbidden by the Mishna.

In the Middle Ages, caterpillar silk was thought to have curative properties. The chief druggist to King Louis XIV of France believed that the phlegm and oil yielded by clue (raw) silk recruited the spirit, and, taken as a powder, purified the blood. The same applied to the shaven head was reckoned very good to cure a vertigo.

It was not until 1860 that eggs of the wild Indian silk moth (*Antheraea*), from which the beautiful Tussah weave is produced, were smuggled into France in a letter via the consular bag. Almost simultaneously a walking stick was carried nonchalantly over the frontier into Belgium with its hollow core stuffed with eggs – forty thousand of which weigh only about one ounce. However, reared in the European climate these moths proved a sad disappointment, for they failed to produce silk of the same matchless quality as that characteristic of the indigenous Indian caterpillar.

James I, who loved novel enterprises, from fishing with cormorants to rearing silk moths, tried to stimulate sericulture in Britain, but it was the refugees from religious and political persecution, generously granted asylum in this country, who were the major factor in the development of our silk industry. Eventually it was reintroduced into India on a modern scale. Certainly no animal has exerted a political or financial influence as great as this silent, voracious, parchment-coloured worm.

Their quiet industry appealed to the poets:

> The worm in silk cocoon
> Stealthily as spider spins,
> As glides the moon.[8]

In a love letter Shelley wrote:

> The silk worm in the dark green mulberry leaves
> His winding sheet and cradle ever weaves.[9]

and Dryden, in a rather different mood, quoted Ovid:

61

> And Worms, that stretch on leaves their filmy Loom,
> Crawl from their Bags and Butterflies become[10]

It is a little difficult to estimate what is the world production of silk today. The survey carried out in 1970 by the Food and Agriculture Association puts the total at around 41,315 metric tons of raw silk, half of which comes from Japan and about a quarter from China.* The Japanese industry is conducted most efficiently and whereas only 2,375,000 workers are required to produce 20,515 metric tons, India employs 3,000,000 farm labourers to produce only 2,250 tons (20,900 dollars' worth of silk textiles). If irrigation and artificial fertilizers are used, 129 kg. of raw silk can be obtained from 1 hectare of mulberry bushes or, expressed differently, 800 to 2,000 dollars' worth of thread. In China today the various stages of silk moth breeding are shared between different communes. Eggs – of which each female lays about 500 – are distributed from a central source, and the rearing of the caterpillars – in large tiered wicker trays – and the cultivation of the mulberry leaves on which they feed are carried out in several separate sub-centres. The cocoons are collected and delivered to the factories, which stifle the chrysalises within the cocoons by heating them to death, de-gum and reel the silk, and subsequently throw or twist it – 'unweave the caterpillar's gluey thread.'[11] Such a factory in the Soochow area receives 200,000 cocoons per 'season' (of which there are four during the summer months) and the caterpillars providing this consignment would have consumed about 4 tons of mulberry leaves.

> Conscious of change the Silkworm Nymphs begin
> Attached to leaves their gluten-threads to spin;
> Then round and round they weave with circling heads
> Sphere within sphere, and form their silken beds[12]

Since each caterpiller can spin about 1,200 metres of reelable silk, turning its head in a figure-of-eight pattern 300,000 times in the process, these cocoons would provide a silken girdle to encompass the earth five times over. In commercial terms one can expect to obtain 448 lbs. of stifled silk (112 lbs. of reeled silk) from 200,000 such cocoons.

Both in China and Japan the domesticated silk moth (*Bombyx mori*) produces white silk. But many varied colours have been obtained from wild

---

* In 1986 the world production of silk had increased by 14,700 metric tonnes of which China produced more than half the grand total of raw silk valued at about $900 million (Tropical Development and Reasearch Institute, 1986).

Female Emperor Moth

AM.3267 <u>bb</u> -'56.

V. A. M.

'. . . *tis but silk that bindeth thee*
Knap the thread and thou art free;
But tis otherwise with me'

species and mutations of the 'tame' type (13 are recorded) are known that produce pale yellow, golden, orange, rusty red, pink, and green silk. The worm its golden woof presents.[13]

The construction of a cocoon is an extremely complicated affair, usually carried out in four successive phases, and the caterpillar reverses the spinning direction at frequencies characteristic for each phase – i.e., the construction of the scaffolding; the outer cocoon; the impregnation of the silk with hindgut exudate of hardening protective crystals, and the inner cocoon. The silk itself is manufactured in the silk glands inside the animal's body, and stored in a reservoir, the ducts of which open to the exterior, on the head of the caterpillar. It consists of a double filament of an insoluble protein, fibroin, embedded in a water-soluble protein called sericin. It seems that its extrusion through the orifice of the gland results in precipitation of the protein and the formation of the semi-crystalline solid fibroin. In other words, on stretching and forcing through the spinnerets, the long, coiled chain molecules of the protein fibrinogen become denatured and unfolded. Mechanical shearing unites reactive groups normally separated by hydration shells. The molecules then assume an orderly crystalline arrangement of the chains. Due to the linking together of the stretched-out molecules, silk fibres are surprisingly strong, stronger in fact when de-gummed than a drawn wire of soft steel of equal diameter. One Chinese species provides extra-strong silk for fishing lines.

> Of golden sands, and crystal brooks
> With silken lines, and silver hooks.[14]

But this filament is taken directly from the caterpillar's glands. Once the larva begins to spin, providing there is traction on the thread, which is essential to the process, it cannot stop, and a continuous flow of secretion pours out – over a mile of it. All the amino acids in silk, with one exception, are secreted in the gland itself, but several are also available in mulberry leaves.

The silkworm can, in some ways, be compared to a chicken. Domestication, in both cases, has led to the loss of functional wings, through unconscious and sometimes conscious selection on the part of man. Unlike its wild relations, the female moth has no well-defined mating season and has lost all restraint; she is permanently on heat, calling continuously for sexual relations. In nature many silk moths are, on the contrary, amazingly fastidious regarding the time and place of intercourse. Thus one of the American silks (*Antheraea polyphemus*) only signals her wish to pair in the presence of a heady emanation from oak leaves (trans-2-hexenal) on which

Contact Thermocardiography

foliage her offspring will feed. Others only copulate at four o'clock sharp in the afternoon. Sometimes the long-distance chemical messages sent out by closely related species of silk moths, and which ensure the meeting of the sexes, are rather similar and therefore might be confusing. The carefully spaced-out mating periods make it certain that there is little or no erroneous hybridization between different species. The emergence of moths from their cocoons at a precise moment of the twenty-four-hour diurnal cycle is the secret of their eventually synchronised love making. In many cases, for instance that of the Chinese oak silk moth (*Antheraea pernyi*), the end of their long sleep within the cocoon is determined by the reception of light

Rothschildia jacobaea

and dark signals by the brain. The cuticle of the pupal case is hard and heavily pigmented, except for a tiny transparent 'window' situated immediately over the brain. The brain in insects is not only the highest centre of the nervous system, but also of the endocrine (hormonal) system. The geometry of the apparently opaque sheltering cocoon is such that it serves as an effective vehicle for the integration of scattered light. The light – the most effective wavelengths extend over the lower region of the visible spectrum including violet, blue, and blue-green – is collected within the cavity of the cocoon and reaches the brain via the glass-like 'pane' at the anterior end of the chrysalis. After the reception of the appropriate light signals, a powerful chemical reagent named cocoonase is released; it wells up round the mouth of the imprisoned moth and gradually wets and melts away the cement-like sericin part of the silk fibres forming the cocoon wall. The flexible fibroin threads are thus freed; the insect pushes them apart with its legs and, at the predetermined moment, creeps out to the amazing contrast of its after-life.

The female silk moth, like the female dog, emits her powerful chemical sex call from a gland at the terminal end of her body. Unlike the bitch, who relies on passive dissemination, she elevates her tail and actively expands and inflates the gland by exerting pressure upon it from within. The scent molecules thus disseminated are carried by air currents to the receptors on the male moth's antennae. These olfactory receptor cells of the domestic silkworm number about 50,000, but in the wild silks there may be as many as 100,000 or more. The male responds by flying upwind along the scent plume, and willy-nilly arrives at the calling female's side, sometimes from only a few yards away but possibly from a distance of several miles.

> . . . The scent
> of the Emperor moth, aflow
> For seven miles around him[15]

So far no biochemist has revealed the chemical structure of dogs' heat scent, but a German scientist extracted the abdominal glands of half a million domestic silk moths and produced 12 milligrams of their purified sex attractant (trans-10,cis-12-hexadecadien-1-ol) which he named 'bombykol.' The male domesticated silk moth responds to this substance by raising its antennae, fluttering its stumpy wings, and marching excitedly upwind – for it cannot fly – and when it arrives at the source of the odour, attempting to copulate with the experimentally impregnated object, whether a piece of filter paper or another male of its own kind. There are, of course, hundreds of different species of moths calling frantically to one another directly darkness falls. It is strange to think how oblivious we are to this concatenation of chemical messages loading the night air, and sometimes the sunny afternoon breezes, with intense sexual stimulation and imperious desire.

The lepidopteran family to which the silks belong contains about fifteen hundred different species, including the largest moths in the world and some of the most beautiful. Their caterpillars are also lovely creatures, adorned with brilliantly coloured fleshy outgrowths or excrescences. Walter Rothschild, the greatest butterfly and moth collector of all time, who had a *faible* for the group – possibly because of their size as well as their aesthetic appeal – had a genus (*Rothschildia*) and a particularly large subspecies (36 cm. from wing-tip to wing-tip) named after him. But they have many other features of interest. Some silk-moth caterpillars are flecked with iridescent gold spots – a combination of structural and physical properties of the cuticle – and impregnated with plant-derived yellow carotenoid pigments; reared on a diet lacking these pigments, the gold is replaced by silver spots. The spines of one species of South American silk-moth caterpillar contain a deadly haemolytic substance, so that chance contact with a broken spine can prove fatal to the person who accidentally touches it. The substance concerned destroys the clotting factor in human blood, and uncontrolled haemorrhage from the mucous membrane of the mouth, nose, and other bodily apertures follows: the victim slowly bleeds to death.

The silks also include among them some of the finest *trompe l'oeil* of nature – moths which in flight and appearance are indistinguishable from dead leaves, including transparent areas in their wings which closely resemble tears in the surface. Birds overlook them, clinging among the foliage of trees, where they merge as if by magic into the background, and ignore them as they drop and flutter earthwards, apparently lifeless leaves wafted hither and thither on a gust of wind.

In recent years an enormous amount of work has been lavished on the silk moths, for they render a melancholy service to mankind as biological tools, as well as the producers of silken thread. In Japan, experimental stations that employ over a thousand research workers and technicians investigate sericulture. The abundance of mutant genes revealed in this species enables scientists working in allied fields to study the biochemical and physiological changes associated with, for instance, the different colours of cocoon silk, the moth's eye – for silk moths are known with black, red, pink, white, green, and lustrous eyes – their eggs and larval and adult integumental patterns. The luckless moths are also exposed to massive radiation research, principally with X-rays, and most of the destructive chromosome aberrations have been induced by this means. Vivisection at all stages of the life-cycle is common practice, and monsters with their brains excised and implanted back into their abdomens, or with bodies tightly ligatured, so that only one half can develop, are an everyday occurrence. The insects inevitably suffer the injection into their bodies of every imaginable chemical substance, from their own hormones to fish poison, tetrodotoxin – one of the most powerful nerve toxins in the world. Recently a scientific magazine cover displayed a beautiful tailed silk moth coupled up to wires linked to an electric recording machine (contact thermocardiography). The heart-beat of this lovely moth was shown to undergo periodic reversal – both backward and forward pulses passing along the aorta. Strangely enough it is assumed by most, if not all scientists – on remarkably slender and dubious evidence – that although insects record 'stress,' they do not feel pain. Possibly the idea originated because there are relatively few cells in the brains of insects, and this suggested – but not on sound scientific evidence – that although they can see, hear, smell, fly, migrate, and so forth, they do all these things

68

like automatons and cannot feel. But the notion seems to have become widely accepted when it became known that moths and butterflies can and do copulate after their heads have been chopped off.

> The Caterpiller on the Leaf
> Repeats to thee thy Mothers grief
> Kill not the Moth nor Butterfly
> For the Last Judgment draweth nigh[16]

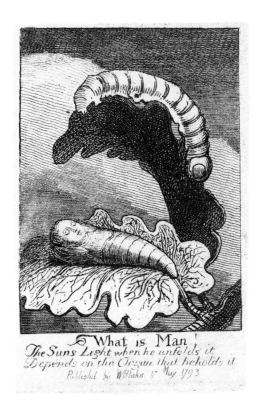

What is Man!
The Suns Light when he unfolds it
Depends on the Organ that beholds it
Published by WBlake 17 May 1793

Harmony in grey and green

Along the Silk Road

The silken thread leads to the star[1]

'When the first party of British tourists stepped down from their coach at the Caves of the Thousand Buddhas,' wrote Peter Hopkirk, 'the last shred of mystery and romance had finally gone from the Silk Road.'[2]

This may well be true, but the Central Asian Desert – six million square miles – remains vast, strange, secretive. If the wind howls over the great sloping dunes it draws up from beneath your feet the 'lui-ing' – the Thunder Roll – which shook and reverberated round Marco Polo's caravan seven hundred years ago.

Burnished by blown sand, a special desert 'flora' of multi-coloured shiny pebbles, rosy pink, veridian green, lilac, apricot, white, vermilion and blue-black basalt glint on the surface of the sand.

In July it is hot and the rain evaporates before it hits the ground. But in autumn the air is clear, and at night the stars are so brilliant and seem so close they might well have been tossed into the air by some local God. They form a luminous mist, a film of glittering diamonds seemingly only just out of reach.

There are still vast areas where the underground waters well up to the surface, and in the foothills of the Tien Shan the desert recedes and one discovers an interlude of green turf, a graceful iris, fritillaries, lupins, and flowering trees with creamy yellow, fragrant blossoms fringing a stream. Suddenly it becomes 'smooth as a moth's nose,'[3] but the foothills are still bare and birds scarce. A few swifts knife past and occasionally a hoopoe twinkles among the bushes – a bird which advertises the fact its flesh is inedible (even to hornets) with its bright, unforgettable plumage. The inevitable buzzards are present – black specks revolving slowly in a remorseless, iron blue sky. The Plain Tiger, the commonest butterfly in the world, suddenly flaps and glides across our path.

In the oasis towns of the Taklamakan and the Gobi deserts, herbalists still lay out their drugs in the medicine shops in the bazaar – pomegranate bark, cinnamon, hyoscyamus, dried poppy heads, gentian and liquorice root. The beautiful sand-jujube tree with its silver leaves and small golden fruit alerts the traveller, far from any beaten track, that water is near. The scent from its tiny creamy flowers is so powerful and penetratingly sweet that

The silken thread leads to the stars

it seeps into your consciousness half a day's ride and many dunes distant from some small oasis.

Towards the Russian border you can still envisage the Silk Road of antiquity – despite the little aeroplanes which ferry travellers from place to place at stategic points along the route, the battered trucks on the Karakoram highway, and the empty beer cans and 'Coca-cola' bottles half hidden in the dust. The people lead pastoral lives: clay-and-wattle houses; felt-covered akois; wooden ploughs; goats; donkeys. Here the curious man-made relationship between camels and the silk moth is much in evidence.

Strangely enough the ancestral camels lived in North America 40 million years ago – animals no bigger than hares, and of course long since extinct. Their importance for the nomadic desert tribes is well illustrated by the fact that in Arabic there are no fewer than one thousand words describing the camel, together with every facet of their lives – from *iaish*, which means camels on which fighting men are mounted, to *bakarah*, a young female.[4]

The camels one meets along the Silk Road today impress one with their sheer indifference and lofty serenity. They are apparently devoid of curiosity. It is difficult to imagine the fits of rage to which the males are subject during the breeding season. Aristotle recorded an enraged camel biting off a man's head. These animals seem to despise the human race and there is no bond between them and their keepers, no trust or manifestations of affection despite their long and intimate association. It is not surprising that the product of the silk moth sent them in thousands half-way round the world, for the camel can travel at ten miles an hour for eighteen hours at a stretch. No other quadruped can equal such a feat of endurance.

The male camel possesses a dulaa. When sexually excited he extrudes this balloon-like organ from the side of his mouth, accompanied by an explosive roar. It looks for all the world like a large piece of pink bubble-gum. Anatomically the dulaa is an inflatable portion of the soft palate, not the tongue. It wobbles strangely from side to side and is no doubt an object of exquisite beauty to the female camel and an unmistakable signal of passion and desire. Another curious habit of the male during the breeding season is a rhythmical lashing of its penis with its own tail, which thus becomes soused in urine, and presently whisked onto the animal's back. Does the urine of camels contain pyrazines like the urine of coyotes? Does it emit some subtle chemical message for the female? We do not know.

It is a strange phenomenon that a yellowish silk thread spun by a rather unimpressive caterpillar should, with the help of this enigmatical quadruped, have at long last established a link between the Western and Eastern worlds. The Silk Road – which really consisted of several roughly parallel routes – once led from Xi'an to Venice. Together the moth and the camel made history for over a thousand years.

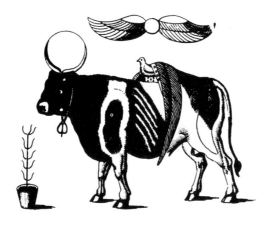

12

The Tale of Liang Shan-po and Zhu Ying-tai

Liang Shan-po was a young scholar living in the Kuai-Ji (now called Shao-Xing), the home town of the late famous writer Lu Xun), a district some 40 miles south-east of Hangchow. When he was sailing on the Qian-Tang River, he met with another young scholar named Zhu Ying-tai on the same boat ferrying across the river. They became good friends and studied side by side for three years.

Liang was a sincere and honest youth. Although he lived with Zhu very intimately for such a long time, he did not suspect that his dear friend was a girl. At that time, under feudal conventions girls were forbidden to study together with boys. The upright, determined and studious Zhu Ying-tai had to study under the guise of a young gentleman. At the end of the third year Liang and Zhu finished their studies and set forth for home. Zhu was a native of Shang-Yu, a district about 20 miles east of Liang's county. The two friends lingered long where they were to part company, loath to say goodbye. Then Zhu told her friend that she had a pretty younger sister. Zhu expected Liang to visit her parents and ask for her sister's hand.

But Liang's visit was delayed because of his appointment as the county magistrate of Jin, a city now called Ningpo about 90 miles east of Hangchow. When he arrived at Zhu's home, he found, to his surprise, that there was no 'younger sister' and the beautiful maiden who came to greet him was no other than Zhu Ying-tai herself. Fancy how happy he was! Liang expressed his everlasting love to his dear friend. With tears in her eyes, Zhu told him that it was too late. Her parents had betrothed her to a man named Ma, the latter living in the county of Jin too.

Rigid feudal decorum forced the two lovers to part. Soon after he returned home, Liang died of a broken heart. And a wedding was to be held for Zhu and Ma, much against Zhu's will. Zhu was sent in a boat to Ma's family for the wedding. There suddenly arose a terrible storm as the boat was drawing near the tomb of Liang Shan-po. It was caught in the storm and Zhu had to land. As soon as she learned that Liang's tomb was there she headed for it unhesitatingly. The tomb opened amidst thunder

A symbol of conjugal happiness

and lightning and Zhu leapt into it. The tomb closed again. Immediately the storm subsided and the sun was shining again. A pair of beautiful butterflies were seen flying out of the tomb, gracefully dancing against the rainbow. They were the spirits of Liang Shan-po and Zhu Ying-tai, united in eternal love after death, ever in defiance of feudal marriage system.

(Translated from the Chinese by Xu Hua-liang)

Whose soul, I wonder?

13

Van Gogh and the Butterflies

Lovely, light as cloud in sky
Butterfly.[1]

We are again assailed by the same tiresome category of sentiments as those associated with quotations from Shakespeare or Proust: why did anyone bother to paint landscapes, grass fields, night skies, stars, trees, after Van Gogh? And so you look with some dismay at the pictures reproduced here. Not only do they fail, miserably, to do justice to the originals, but they devalue all the rest.

Van Gogh described his little pear tree in blossom with the Brimstone butterfly tangled in its branches:

> . . . The ground violet, in the background a wall with straight poplars and a very blue sky. The little pear tree has a violet trunk and white flowers, with a big yellow butterfly on one of the clusters.[2]

Van Gogh, too, was enamoured of white butterflies and two of his most attractive and touching canvases match Neruda's poetry for sheer romance – white wings caught among the stalks of green corn and poppies, or fluttering among great tussocks of coarse grass. But the world's most painfully beautiful picture is 'The Prison Courtyard' – the very antithesis of flowering hayfields and sunlit wings. Like Shakespeare, who founded many of his plays on some fairly well-known popular theme or tale, Van Gogh based this picture on a reasonably dull, rather pedestrian engraving by the artist Gustave Doré.[3] The picture shows us the grey, lumpish, depressed prisoners exercising in a small circle, watched by a group of erect guards and surrounded by towering grey prison walls. High, high above their heads two white butterflies dip and flirt in airy freedom. No-one has noticed them.

It is a terrible picture, steeped in misery and degradation – a profound indictment of humanity. The white butterflies – the distilled essence of every white butterfly that has emerged from a chrysalis – are there to remind us of paradise.

The light of a butterfly's wing lying on the arches of a cathedral . . .

14

Marcel Proust – Naturalist

More white and red than doves and roses are.[1]

Marcel Proust is the first and greatest urban naturalist the world has ever known – the others have yet to be born.

Unfortunately, if you include Shakespeare or Proust in an anthology you destroy everything else. Once you read:

So shows a snowy dove trooping with crows. . . .[2]

or

The pigeons, whose beautiful iridescent bodies, (shaped like hearts, and, surely, the lilacs of the feathered kingdom) . . .[3]

you put the book aside. The rest suddenly becomes superfluous.

Proust is unlikely ever to have tramped across fields, or pushed his way along overgrown woodland paths, or climbed a five-barred gate, or even got his feet damp in long grass. His natural history came to him, miraculously, resting on his bed in a seaside hotel, or in a Paris drawing-room, or crossing the park surrounded by screaming children and barking dogs, or from the closed window of a cab, or the kitchen, or in Church. His apple blossom was purchased from the florist. . . .

He wrote this paragraph in his bedroom at Cambray:

. . . my room which trembled with the effort to defend its frail, transparent coolness against the afternoon sun, behind its almost closed shutters through which, however, a reflection of the sunlight had contrived to slip in on its golden wings, remaining motionless between glass and woodwork, in a corner, like a butterfly poised upon a flower.[4]

And this, after returning from a dutiful Sunday afternoon walk with his parents:

Elsewhere a corner seemed to be reserved for the commoner kinds of lily; of a neat pink or white like rocket-flowers, washed clean like porcelain, with housewifely care; while a little further again, were others, pressed close together in a floating garden-bed, as though pansies had flown out of a garden like butterflies and were hovering with blue and burnished wings over the transparent shadowiness of this watery border.[5]

Ships reminded him of butterflies, moths . . . flies . . . In this instance he was contemplating a canvas in the artist's studio:

> . . . The continuity of the ocean was suggested only by the gulls which, wheeling over what seemed to be solid rock, were as a matter of fact inhaling the moist vapour of the shifting tide. Other laws were discernibly in the same canvas, as, at the foot of the immense cliffs, the lilliputian grace of white sails on the blue mirror on whose surface they looked like butterflies asleep and certain contrasts between the depth of the shadows and the pallidity of the light.[6]

Dining in a fashionable restaurant, he watched the sunset:

> The sun crept down the sky and set in the sea, through the glass panels of the great dining-room, behind which, at the hour when the light died, the motionless wings of vessels, smoky blue in the distance, looked like exotic and nocturnal moths in a show-case.[7]

Proust not infrequently selected preserved butterflies for comparison:

> Her eyes shone like, in a matrix in which the opal is still embedded, the two facets which alone have as yet been polished, which, become more brilliant than metal, reveal, in the midst of the blind matter that encumbers them, as it were the mauve, silken wings of a butterfly placed under glass.[8]

On this occasion he was in bed in Paris:

> Meanwhile winter was at an end; the fine weather returned, and often when Albertine had just bidden me good night, my room, my curtains, the wall above the curtains being still quite dark, in the nuns' garden next door I could hear, rich and precious in the silence like a harmonium in church, the modulation of an unknown bird which, in the Lydian mode, was already chanting matins, and into the midst of my darkness flung the rich dazzling note of the sun that it could see. Once indeed, we heard all of a sudden the regular cadence of a plaintive appeal. It was the pigeons beginning to coo.[9]

> The resemblance between their cooing and the crow of the cock was as profound and as obscure as, in Vinteuil's septet, the resemblance between the theme of the adagio and that of the closing piece, which is based upon the same key-theme as the other. . . . So this melancholy fragment performed by the pigeons was a sort of cockcrow in the minor, which did not soar up into the sky, did not rise vertically, but, regular

as the braying of a donkey, enveloped in sweetness, went from one pigeon to another along a single horizontal line, and never raised itself, never changed its laterial plaint . . .[10]

Then again he felt the sun and the rain through his Paris bedroom window:

I had discovered one of those tempestuous, discordant, delightful days when the roofs, soaked by an occasional shower and dried by a breath of wind or a ray of sunshine let fall a cooing eavesdrop, and, as they wait for the wind to resume its turn preen in the momentary sunlight that has burnished them their pigeon's breast of slates.[11]

Proust was the supreme master, with the pen, of time passing and change – the diurnal as well as the annual cycle. He appreciated the significance of clouds moving over the sun, of the glare at high noon, of the wind, warm and rustling, of cool breezes at nightfall, the last peals of thunder growling among the lilac trees.[12] He had the most vital of all gifts for a naturalist: a profound and sensitive understanding of the weather.

'The favourite signature of the Master of Chelsea'

'*A profound and sensitive understanding of the weather*'

15

Neruda and the Butterfly of Shadow

Neruda's doves and butterflies, even in translation, are overwhelmingly romantic.

> The Spring I love
> The moon above the desert
> The breast of the wild dove[1]

Oh my sad love, your smile is like a butterfly opening its wings.[2]

> The butterfly awaits your gaze
> The seagull lights up the water for you
> There are two halves of the world:
> The blue fire and the expanse of ocean.[3]

> Albertina Rose
> Butterfly,
> Necklace that dazzles
> All things.[4]

But had he seen Blake's illustration to *The Marriage of Heaven and Hell?*[5] He wrote:

> A butterfly of shadow has come to sleep on your belly.[6]

Possibly he has explained this somewhere – I simply do not know. Or is it just a Zhivago-like coincidence?

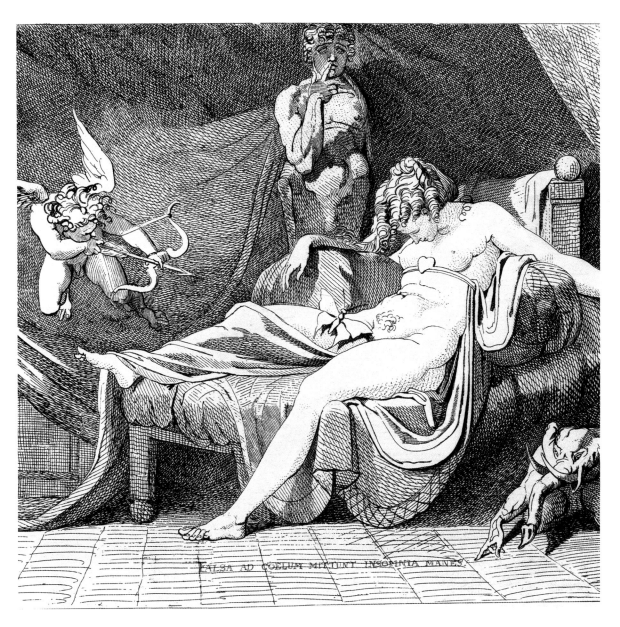

A butterfly of shadow has come to sleep on your belly

The Lybian lion hunts no butterflies

16

Hunting Butterflies

The Lybian lion hunts no butterflies[1]

How Happier is that Flea
Which in thy Breast doth playe,
Than that pied Butterflie
Which courts the Flame and in the same doth die.[2]

This verse by William Drummond links fleas and butterflies – I know no other which catches my two favourite insects in such a fine net.

I searched in vain for a moth flying round the candle in Georges de La Tour's marvellous picture of the woman – presumably undressing on her way to bed – hunting a flea. And sadly, Donne's poem in which the lovers' lifeblood mingles romantically within the insect's proventriculous – 'cloystered in these living walls of Jet'[3] – lacks all trace of gilded wings (someone once described a flea as a speck of tobacco with a spring). But there is no picture of a butterfly hunt which you remember in every fervent detail, or which can compare with the concentrated magic and homely sensuality of the woman 'purpling her naile in blood of innocence.'[4]

A different chase took place above the Dead Sea, when David stood on the top of an hill afar off[5] and cried out to Saul: 'For the king of Israel is come out to seek a flea, as when one doth hunt a partridge in the mountains.'[6]

Words, said Hazlitt, are the only things that last for ever.[7] Curiously enough the memory of butterfly hunting survives far better than many more significant moments in a long life, or many memorable words of wisdom, for it is generally associated with childhood – the time when summer days are always sunny and warm. It can be extremely difficult, if well nigh impossible, to recall what happened last Monday but the day, half a century since, when we caught a Purple Emperor, is clear as crystal. Natural selection has seen to it that what we learn as children lasts a lifetime, when we are old, what happened yesterday is of little significance to the survival of the species.

Sometimes we find butterflies, especially the Danaids, shown as wonderful, decorative asides in Egyptian hunting scenes – for instance, those from the Tomb of Nebamun at Thebes[8] – but the earliest record I know of a genuine butterfly hunt is the group of enthusiastic boys flying their tethered

Boys with Butterflies

specimens – which includes a bird, a goldfinch – in the pages of the early-14th-century Queen Mary Psalter.

> Behold how eager this our little boy
> Is for a butterfly, as if all joy
> All profits, honour, yea, and lasting pleasures
> Were wrapped up in her.[9]

In another 14th-century manuscript, 'The Romance of Alexander,' we find a painting of energetic ladies in long skirts chasing butterflies with bell-shaped nets.

The Encyclopaedia of Traditional Symbols tells us that the butterfly shown in some mediaeval paintings, clasped in the hand of the Infant Jesus, symbolises eternity, the insect's stages of development being life and death and resurrection. But when we see a colfox, 'full of sly iniquitee' – bright red with neat black points – (watched by the cock who cast his eye 'among the wortes on a boterflye')[10], leap to snap at a Cabbage White flapping past in the sunshine, we are suddenly aware of something in our genes – older than any religion, primitive, archaic – which compels us to strive after the winged insect. It is like catching sunbeams linked to a fleeting, secret, and mysterious moment of unalloyed happiness.

There is difficulty, however, even for a prose poet like Nabokov to share the experience of entomological discovery with more than a narrow field of specialists. Much the same problem confronts the dedicated gardener. Unless his or her reader knows *Iris danfordia* and *Viola hirta* from personal experience, the cumbersome Latin names convey nothing of significance and merely ruin the prose flow. The poignant needle-thin yellow of the baby iris, and the surprisingly luminous blue element in the mauve flower of the hairy violet are totally lost in the verbiage. Similarly you must see for yourself the electric brilliance of *Morpho cypris*, a drifting fragment of sunny sky,[11] before you can be deeply moved by the description of its undulating, glittering flight and fleeting azure presence. Gossip about friends, we know, is delectable, but about strangers is boring beyond belief. The nostalgic delight of a remembered butterfly hunt, with its mixture of lovely landscapes, summer grasses, dappled sunlight, scientific discovery, and the primitive enjoyment of the chase, is reserved for fellow entomologists. The great Alfred Wallace realised this when he described the capture of a great Bird Wing, one of the most gorgeously coloured butterflies in the world:

> Fine specimens of the male are more than seven inches across the wings, which are velvety black and fiery orange . . . The beauty and brilliance of the insect are indescribable and none but a naturalist can understand the intense excitement I experienced . . . On taking it out of my net and opening the glorious wings my heart began to beat violently, the blood rushed to my head and I felt more like fainting than I have done when in apprehension of immediate death. I had a headache the rest of the day.[12]

A great naturalist of his time confided to his wife that when, as a young man, he suddenly came upon a crowd of brilliant swallowtails flickering to and fro in a forest clearing in Ceylon, his admiration and excitement were so intense he experienced a violent erection.

The more absurd aspect of the sober, adult man galumphing along after a fragile insect, skimming like a winged flower in the sunshine was well described in *Coriolanus*:

> I saw him run after a gilded butterfly; and when he caught it, he let it go again; and after it again; and over and over he comes, and up again; catched it again; and whether his fall enraged him, or how 'twas, he did so set his teeth, and tear it; O, I warrant, how he mammocked it![13]

Alexander Pope described the chase in a more sophisticated vein:

> Of all th' enamel'd race, whose silv'ry wing
> Waves to the tepid Zephyrs of the spring,
> Or swims along the fluid atmosphere,
> Once brightest shin'd the child of Heat and Air.
> I saw, and started from its vernal bow'r
> The rising game, and chac'd from flow'r to flow'r
> It fled, I follow'd; now in hope, now pain;
> It stopt, I stopt; it mov'd, I mov'd again.
> At last it fix'd, 'twas on what plant it pleas'd,
> And where it fix'd, the beauteous bird I seiz'd:
> Rose or Carnation was below my care;
> I meddle, Goddess: only in my sphere
> I tell the naked fact without disguise,
> And, to excuse it, need but shew the prize;
> Whose spoils this paper offers to your eye,
> Fair ev'n in death: this peerless Butterfly.[14]

Nabokov adored the ecstasy of pursuit in a natural habitat but he also thought it great fun locating a new species among the broken insects in an old biscuit tin sent over by a sailor from some remote island. Spotting a perfect *Vanessa atalanta* concealed in a Brueghel bush thrilled him almost as much as spotting a rare mutant on the wing.[15]

Virginia Woolf was a great lover of moths and among her collected essays is a nostalgic description of children 'sugaring' by the light of a lantern:

About an hour previously, several pieces of flannel soaked in rum and sugar had been pinned to a number of trees. The business of dinner now engrossing the grown-up people we made ready our lantern, our poison jar and took our butterfly net in our hands. The road that skirted the wood was so pale that its hardness grated upon our boots unexpectedly. It was the last strip of reality, however, off which we slipped into the gloom of the unknown. The lantern shoved its wedge of light through the dark as though the air were a black snow piling itself up in banks on either side of the yellow beam . . . The light was turned very cautiously towards the tree, first it rested upon the grass at the foot, then it mounted a few inches of the trunk, as it mounted our excitement became more and more intense, then it gradually enveloped the flannel and the cataracts of falling treacle. As it did so several wings flitted around us. . . . The scarlet underwing was already there, immobile as

The painter's daughters chasing a butterfly

before astride a vein of sweetness, drinking deep. Without waiting a second this time the poison pot was uncovered and adroitly manoeuvred so that as he sat there the moth was covered and escape cut off. There was a flash of scarlet within the glass. Then he composed himself with folded wings. He did not move again.[16]

*

Only very rarely do we find in butterfly literature a link with human sentiment. You look in vain for love among the butterflies in Patrick Matthews' anthology of collecting. Even Miss Fountaine's contribution to that delightful compilation lacks her usual romantic flavour. Like the average lepidopterist she is more concerned with the weather, which 'was hopelessly bad' and having seen nothing on Mount Olympus but dense clouds of vapours, she returned to Broussa drenched to the skin. Evelyn Cheesman's butterfly hunting in the Cyclops Mountains was also marred by the climate.

> Incessant moisture was more and more oppressive . . . the moist heat depresses the nerves after a while, then one cannot sleep and is never free of headache.[17]

Miss Cheesman broke camp when she found a leech in the teapot. . . .

Romance, however, crept into the discovery of a place in the Hâute Savoie where *Erebia* – the mountain ringlet – flew in thousands, like a never-ending thin black snow-storm.

> The butterflies covered the white walls of this deserted cottage, which had been left in ruins after a battle with the Resistance during the last weeks of the war. There they sat, beading the stucco, their wings spread towards the sun – so close together their shadows mingled, and in numbers that were almost horrifying. Clavière was a frontier village which had suffered from a series of small but bloody battles, and large areas of the mountain forests had been destroyed and were now a mass of ragged, torn stumps. The old lady with a raven on her shoulder, who kept the Inn – the one intact building in Clavière at that time – had lost four sons in the conflict. Only the ruined ski-lift, which festooned the lower slopes, trailing on the ground between the drunken posts, reminded one of a more prosperous past. You could walk for hours in the mountains and never meet a soul, except for a rare smuggler, in city clothes, carrying a battered *attaché* case, who enquired anxiously if you knew the whereabouts of the frontier posts.

'Behold, how eager this our little boy . . .'

Clavière now belonged to the butterflies. The uncut, flowering alpine haymeadows starred with pink Dianthus, and the huge tattered clearings in the woods seemed to suit them and they swarmed up from your feet – Clouded Yellows, Whites, Apollos and Swallowtails – as you passed, to add to the thin concourse of ringlets which enveloped and flickered round you on all sides.

It was the first time I had visited the mountains since the war – it was the Elysian fields and I was glad my net was merely symbolical and I was watching, not collecting.

Phyllis was a dedicated walker and as sure-footed as a mountain goat, but she was not interested in butterflies. She once confessed she hated dawdling, and preferred running along these green precipitous paths – feeling the mountain air blowing through her hair, with a hint of snow crystals and sun. Phyllis had light brown hair and widely set grey eyes, which protruded very slightly with the beautiful gaze of a startled moufflon. Now she walked rapidly ahead and I noticed with affectionate amusement that whereas my white shorts were free of curious insect visitors, her grey skirt – the colour no doubt reminiscent of the local dusky mules – was immensely attractive, and her delightful backside was plastered with ugly, grey horseflies. In fact some beasts of burden must have recently passed that way, although we had neither seen or heard them. They had left their droppings along the path, which were now garlanded with a jewel-like assembly of butterflies – skippers, blues, coppers and fritillary-like species, feeding drunkenly on the semi-liquid manure:

<blockquote>
thou didst drink
The stale of horses and the gilded puddle
Which beasts would cough at;[18]
</blockquote>

I popped my net over a little heap and caught two or three score. Phyllis came back to exclaim with wonder. I looked at her. Would the distance between the brisk walker and the butterfly dawdler, I wondered, increase with time? Or would it dwindle? One of the fritillaries resettled on her arm, unrolled its tongue, and began to probe her sunburn lotion. Another followed suit. I kissed her shadowed eyelids as she looked down at them. 'They are short of salt, I think at this altitude,' I said, unromantically, 'They are after your sweat. By the way – will you marry me?' Yes, said Phyllis, she thought she would.

The ringlets continued to flicker past without a pause.[19]

94

17

Yellow Butterflies

These little yellow butterflies may know;
With falling leaves they waver to and fro . . .[1]

Yellow butterflies have a special attraction for both poets and entomologists. Frederic Prokosch claims that Nabokov imagined himself a lemon-coloured Swallowtail:

> . . . to feel the air skimming under my outstretched wings (he said), to feel the leaves caressing my scales, to hear the petals under my proboscis, to feel the coming of autumn in the depth of my thorax and the scent and far off storm in the beads of my antennae. And also to feel the delight of the larvae as it gnaws at the nettles and the delicious growth of wings in the depth of a cocoon. That's what it means to be a butterfly: an entire labyrinth of ecstasies.[2]

Prokosch of course was paraphrasing and misquoting Nabokov. Butterflies don't spin cocoons nor does the larva of this species eat nettles, but I have no doubt the butterfly-hunting poet often imagined the Yellow Swallowtail's world. He described how, as a boy, his guiding angel pointed out to him a rare visitor:

> . . . a splendid, pale yellow creature with black blotches, blue crenels, and a cinnabar eyespot above each chrome-rimmed black tail. As it probed the inclined flower from which it hung, its powdery body slightly bent, it kept restlessly jerking its great wings, and my desire for it was one of the most intense I have ever experienced.[3]

Every butterfly and moth in the world carries yellow pigments – carotenoids – in its body. Neither they nor we can manufacture them ourselves and we depend absolutely on plants, directly or indirectly, for our supply of this vitally important element, but since plants produce 100 million tons per year, they are available on a lavish scale. Caterpillars themselves secrete blue bile pigments but they sequester and store the yellow pigments from their food plant, and the two mix in the eye of the beholder to produce the characteristic cryptic green body colour of the caterpillar. Reared in the laboratory, on a carotenoid-free diet, they are sky-blue in colour and the silk they spin for their chrysalis-girdle is then snow-white.

In a sense the yellow pigments rule our world, for without them there would be no light. They are the source of Vitamin A, which in turn plays a key role in the synthesis of the visual pigment, rhodopsin. These excitations, wrote George Wald, throughout their entire range appear to be derived chemically from a single closely-knit family of compounds, the carotenoids. This relationship persists from phototropism in moulds to vision in man.[4] The link between us and dawn is plant life.

And the wild asses did stand in the high places, they snuffed up the wind like dragons; their eyes did fail because there was no grass.[5]

Jeremiah grasped the connection.

Fortunately these yellow pigments are generously displayed for us to marvel at – in oranges and lemons, baby chicks, egg yolks, saffron, goldfish, canaries, pollen, ripening corn, autumn leaves, cream, the gonads of starfish, sponges, the retina of hens' eyes, honey, the hind wings of locusts, the carapace of lobsters, buttercups and daisies and: 'Sulphur butterflies on the purple flowers Flattened like victims . . .'[6]

In Florida at dawn, they are the only species on the wing, noiseless yellow butterflies[7] with a coal-black rim to their wings, fluttering unobtrusively an inch above the soil, looking presumably for the appropriate green leaf on which to lay their eggs. Nina Epton records a brilliant yellow butterfly crossing a brick-red path but her eye lighted still more eagerly on a bird-sized all-black butterfly, poised like a velvet bow on a waxy white orchid.[8] Both the French poet Gérard de Nerval and Marcel Proust also seem hooked on contrasting black and yellow:

> *Voici le papillon faune*
> *Noir et jaune.*[9]

Marcel Proust was incurably romantic. When Madame de Guermantes – with whom he was deeply in love – spoke to him (the narrator) of the Arpajon drawing room, he mused:

I saw a yellow butterfly – and in the Swann drawing-room . . . a black butterfly, its wings powdered with snow.[10]

And at dusk Peter Russell remarked that:

Moths fly in through the windows on summer nights full of news,
With scalloped lemon-pale wings with narrow bars,
Swallow-tailed with long questioning antennae
And gleaming crystal eyes. . . .[11]

Yellow Butterfly

'The highest enjoyment of timelessness is when I stand among rare butterflies and their food plants'

Next morning, leaning out of the window and looking towards the distant hills:

> An omnibus across the bridge
> Crawls like a yellow butterfly [12]

And then after the Sabbath prayers:

> The Baal Shem's butterfly
> Followed me down the hill,
> Now the Baal Shem is dead
> These hundreds of years
> And a butterfly ends its life
> In three flat-swept days.
> So this was a miracle,
> Dancing down all these wars and truces
> Yellow as a first-day butterfly,
> Nothing of time or massacre
> In its bright flutter.
>
> Now the sharp stars are in the sky
> And I am shivering as I did last night,
> And the wind is not warmer
> For the yellow butterfly
> Folded somewhere on a sticky leaf
> And moving like a leaf itself.
> And how truly great
> A miracle this is, that I,
> Who this morning saw the Baal Shem's butterfly
> Doing its glory in the sun,
> Should spend this night in darkness,
> Hands pocketed against the flies and cold. [13]

In *One Hundred Years of Solitude* Gabriel García Márquez describes a plague of yellow butterflies. He tells us how Meme Buendia, the daughter of one of the founding families of Macondo, was enjoying an illicit love affair with Mauricio Babilonia, a local garage mechanic. Her mother, Fernanda, disapproved furiously because of the man's inferior social position.

It was then Meme noticed the yellow butterflies that always heralded the appearance of Mauricio Babilonia. She had seen them before, in particular at the petrol station, and she had assumed that they were drawn by the smell of paint there. Sometimes she had sensed them fluttering about his head in the half-light of the cinema. But when Mauricio Babilonia began to pursue her, like a spectre only visible to her in the midst of the multitude, she understood that these yellow butterflies were in some way connected to him. Mauricio Babilonia was always in the audiences that thronged concerts, the cinema, high mass, and she did not have to see him to know this, because the butterflies betrayed him. Once in the cinema Aureliano the Second [Meme's father] grew so impatient with the suffocating throng of their wings that Meme felt an impulse to confide in him, as she had promised, but her instinct told her that this time he would not laugh as usual: 'What would your mother say if she only knew!' One morning, whilst they were pruning the roses, Fernanda screamed and pulled Meme away from the spot where she stood, which was the very spot where Remedios the Fair ascended into heaven. For a moment she believed the miracle was about to be repeated by her own daughter, having been disturbed by a flutter of wings. It was the butterflies. Meme saw them as if they had that instant been born in the light, and her heart leapt into her mouth. At that moment Mauricio Babilonia walked into the garden with a small parcel which he said was a present from Patricia Brown. Meme stifled her blushes, calmed herself, and even managed to smile unselfconsciously, telling him to leave the parcel on the verandah since her hands were grubby. The only thing Fernanda noticed about the man whom a few months later she was to throw out of the house without even realising she had seen him before, was the bilious texture of his skin.

'He's a very strange man,' said Fernanda. 'One can see in his face that he is about to die.'

Meme assumed her mother had been affected by the sight of the butterflies. But her affair was subsequently discovered. Henceforth, she was banned from meeting Mauricio Babilonia and confined within the house. Tragedy followed:

The yellow butterflies invaded the house at twilight. Every evening on emerging from the bathroom, Meme would find Fernanda in a state of despair, slaughtering butterflies with the insecticide can. 'This is a misfortune,' she would say, 'all my life I have been told that butterflies at night bring bad luck.' One night, whilst Meme was in the bath, Fernanda chanced to walk into her bedroom, and found so many butterflies there she could scarcely breathe. . . . This time she did not wait for an appropriate occasion, as she had before. The next day she invited the new mayor to lunch and asked him to set up a nocturnal sentry in the forecourt of the house, because she was under the impression that her hens were being poached. That night the sentry laid low Mauricio Babilonia in the act of clambering through the roof into the bathroom where Meme waited for him, naked and trembling with love among the butterflies, as she had done every night for the past few months. A bullet lodged in his spine, paralysed him and confined him to his bed for the rest of his days. He died of age and isolation, tormented by his memories and the yellow butterflies who never gave him a moment's peace . . .[14]

Yellow butterflies themselves – any more than the hapless Babilonia – are not shielded from misfortune. They are great migrants and follow primaeval uncharted routes, which they have taken for thousands of years, ignoring the march of time, the destruction of forests, and the dangers of dual carriageways and motorised transport.

'. . . as we dipped down into a low-lying tropical valley,' wrote Irene Nicholson, 'we ran into a cloud of yellow butterflies, solid as butter. The bus cut relentlessly through them, and it was sad to see, at our next stopping place, that the radiator was powdered all over with fine yellow dust from the broken wings.'[15]

Pablo Neruda witnessed one of these migrating clouds blown relentlessly out to sea by a hurricane:

> While the sad wind goes slaughtering butterflies
> I love you . . .[16]

The Annunciation

18

The Winged Conjunction

> Fistfuls of butterflies, flung on
> the air like doves,
> Snowflaked the garden, bewildered
> and dazed by the heat.[1]

Although butterflies are, in man's subconscious if not his conscious mind, symbols of the soul, and doves symbols of the spirit, these two are rarely found coupled in our poetry and pictures.

Call us what you will, wee are made such by love, says Donne:

> Call her one, mee another flye,
> We are Tapers too, and at our owne cost die,
> And wee in us finde the Eagle and the Dove.[2]

Neruda, who like Donne knew about love, joined the fly and the bird in an unforgettable poem which we have unashamedly plundered for our title. For here the silent fluttering soul is given its moment of despairing eloquence.

> I like for you to be still, and you seem far away. It sounds as though you were lamenting, a butterfly cooing like a dove.[3]

Lewis Belrose is frankly sentimental:

> How sweet to listen to the Dove
> When all the rest forget to sing,
> And watch the swallows wantoning,
> And butterflies, the gold whereof
> Comes sinking through the skies above
> Like feathers from an angel's wings.[4]

Sometimes in a Book of Hours one finds the bird of snow and golden icicles 'oaring down mid-air from Heaven'[5] into the centre of a page to greet the Virgin, while the illuminated border is unexpectedly full of bright flowers and wonderfully realistic Meadow Browns and Wall butterflies. Occasionally a Cabbage White or a Magpie moth is popped in among the pink petals, revealing with delightful clarity the artist's careful concern for

Le Moult

earthly rather than celestial matters. But why the Satyrids – the browns
– are habitually selected in preference to the more flamboyant Nymphalids
– the Purple Emperors or the Red and White Admirals, or even the sharp
little blues – is a riddle we would dearly like to solve.

The winged conjunction

'I will be more jealous of thee than a Barbary cock-pigeon over his hen'

19

Captive Spirits

Sitting in the sun under the dove-house wall[1]

When many animals were required for sacrifice they were reared in captivity to meet this urgent demand. The Jews in biblical times bred doves – almost certainly for this purpose. Isaiah asked, Who are these that fly as a cloud, and as the doves to their windows?[2] We may deduce that dovecotes in those days were constructed much as they are now, with rows of separate little entrances from which the birds could subsequently look out and survey the world, well sheltered from the lurking falcon.

We know that doves were sold in the Temple, presumably to those who wished to perform ritual sacrifices of purification or expiation. Jesus, it will be recalled, turned over the chairs of 'them that sold doves'[3] and John recorded that He said unto them . . . Take these things hence. . . .[4] Before 3000 B.C., in the IVth Egyptian Dynasty, pigeons figured in a bill of fare.[5] They may also have been eaten by the Israelites.*

The Romans built pigeon lofts on the summit of large tombs – why, we do not know – while in mediaeval times dovecotes were frequently erected alongside graveyards – in this case with a view to assisting the spirit as it left the body in the form of a dove. Still later when, during the winter, there was a scarcity of fresh meat in England, the pigeon became a culinary delicacy reserved for the landed gentry. In Milton's day all the big estates had their dovecotes and there were said to be no fewer than 25,000 in the country, housing from 500 to 1,000 birds each. Some of these were built in the continental manorial style as circular towers with a revolving ladder, or potence, within. Probably the oldest standing dovecote in England is the small church tower at Saresfield Court, erected in the first half of the 13th century.

. . . I saw the pigeon towers
Streaked white with dung, and goat-kids born in blood.[6]

Paracelsus claimed that if you buried gold in pigeon's dung, it increased. . . .

---

*Bodenheimer (*Animal and Man in Bible Lands*) categorically denies this.

Blake abhorred captive birds:

> A Dove house filled with Doves and Pigeons
> Shudders Hell thro' all its regions.[7]

But the observant Haiku master is gently philosophical:

> The caged dove spreads one wing
> Basking in the winter sun.[8]

In Scotland none could build a dovecote unless he possessed land to a yearly value of no less than 'ten chalders of victuals' — and then only one. Similarly, in France the dovecote right was a privilege of the nobility, although if you owned twenty-six *arpens* (about 100 perch) of land you were allowed a single wooden dovecote, but restricted to no more than 120 nesting boxes. However, the French Revolution put an end to the feudal rights of French pigeon fanciers.

In the United States, modern commercial squab production is greater than in any European country — today about 100,000 birds are reared annually for home consumption.

During World War II wild wood-pigeons were considered an agricultural pest and simultaneously a useful addition to British food ration. Free cartridges were issued to marksmen. About 5 or 6 million of these birds — a meat supply of around 3,000 tons — were flying around Britain at the time. A million or more reached the meat market every year, mostly shot coming to decoys in the spring. I always remember the crop of one dead bird, amidst the massive slaughter at central market, which was split open and crammed with fresh, shining buttercup flowers in full bloom.

Long before the rise of Judaism or Christianity, and even longer before we began consuming these beautiful birds, pigeons and doves were kept in captivity and also revered and esteemed in many parts of the world. In the annals of the Pharaoh Thothmes III (about 1500 B.C.) mention is made of 258 pairs of pigeons and '5,237 pigeons of another kind.' Wendell Levi tells us: This adoration (which originated with the fertility cult of the Goddess Astarte) extended from the Sumerians, Accadians, etc. to the Assyrians, Phoenicians, the Persians and the Hindus and later the Mohammedans.[9] The hundreds of pigeons nesting on and around the Mosque of the Doves in Constantinople are left unmolested and are considered sacred even today. In big cities in the Western world, they are considered pests, damaging the historic buildings with their droppings, and their numbers are reduced with the aid of narcotic or sterilizing chemically treated baits.

The Festival of St Swithin

'I will be more jealous of thee than a Barbary cock-pigeon over his hen'[10] said Rosalind to Orlando. But nobody knows who first imported that Shakespearean breed to England, or where it originated. Possibly an exiled Persian took it with him to Africa in the 14th century when Timour the Tartar conquered Persia; it is something the refugee would have valued extremely highly.

Today most old-fashioned farmhouses still keep a few pigeons in the yard. The flock may have begun as a single pure-bred variety, White Fantails or the domesticated Rock Dove, but very soon the passing stranger is drawn into the little party – a Magpie Tumbler turns up and settles down, and then a vigorous fawn-and-white cock of no known breed appears, stamps his progeny, and in no time the new arrivals and their offspring have obscured the aristocratic lineage of the founder flock.

Time as he passes us has a dove's wing

Therefore do nimble-pinion'd doves draw Love [11]

They can be observed from the farmhouse:

> I looked at the pigeons down in the kitchen yard. . . . They look like
> little gay juds by shape when they walk, strutting and jod-jodding with
> their heads. The two young ones are all white and the pins of the folded
> wings, quill pleated over quill, are like crisp and shapely cuttleshells
> found on the shore. The others are dull thundercolour, or black-grape-
> colour, except in the white pieings, the quills and tail, and in the shot
> of the neck. I saw one up on the eaves of the roof: as it moved its head
> a crush of satin green came and went, a wet or soft flaming of the light. [12]

Some time during the morning the pigeons usually rise with a clatter,
wheel off into the sky, and depart towards the fields to forage on stubble
or among the young peas.

Occasionally one individual elects to stay behind.

. . . on cobbled yards, among the loose dung and the warm straw
smelling of horse-piss, walks one white pigeon.[13]

When the doves have left, the farmyard seems lifeless and utterly bereft.
But when in the late afternoon 'Sun-steeped in fire the homeward pinions
sway,'[14] everything seems restored. Quite irrationally there suddenly
appears a good reason why the dove was chosen as a symbol of the Holy
Spirit. Strange bird . . .

St Francis preaching to the birds

20

Sweet Little Red Feet! Why Did You Die . . . ?[1]

Why do so many white birds have red feet? This is the sort of problem with which one might well occupy one's mind, with one eye on the lights, in traffic jams. But Alpine Choughs, which are as black as coal, also possess coral legs. They roost in mountain caves above the snow line where the temperature at night falls to minus thirty degrees Fahrenheit. Miraculously, or so it seems, their feet are not turned into blocks of ice. Why do not the red webbed soles of sea-gulls, standing on the frozen ponds in St. James's Park, succumb to frostbite?

> But what gives me most joy is when I see
> Snow on my doorstep, printed by their feet.[2]

But are these marks of suffering? Are hungry sparrows in winter like the little mermaid, treading eternally on icy knives? The physiologists tell us that heat loss in birds is dissipated most readily through the naked feet. In fact when they get too hot some storks deposit fluid excreta on their long red legs to increase evaporative heat loss. To combat cold they shunt blood rapidly through their feet, shutting off the fine capillaries and anastomosing their veins and arteries. Scientists in their own curious free-verse type of English describe their conclusions thus: The A-V (*arteriovenous*) shunt flow is controlled by a synergistic neurogenic mechanism involving both a cholinergic vasodilator and an adrenergic vasoconstrictor component.[3]

Gulls, in cold weather, we have noticed, pull up first one leg and then the other into their feathery breasts. The tropical species of doves with fleshy extremities suffer terribly from cold when brought to Europe to adorn our aviaries, for pigeons, whether woodies or turtles, are truly birds of high summer. They are noted walking with sticky feet upon the green crowns of almond trees[4] and 'paddling in the sunshine where the trees are as bright as a shower of broken glass.'[5] There is nothing in the world so evocative of a June day as the moan of doves in immemorial elms[6], and yet so strangely melancholy.

> How often these hours, have I heard the
> monotonous crool of a dove –

Voice low, insistent, obscure, since its nest
    it has hid in a grove –
Flowers of the linden where through the host of
    the honeybees rove.
And I have been busily idle; no problems;
    nothing to prove;
No urgent foreboding; but only life's shallow
    habitual groove:
Then why, if I pause to listen, should the
    languageless note of a dove
So dark with disquietude seem? And what is it
    sorrowing of?[7]

There is a legend among the Rengma Nagas that the Green Magpie got its scarlet shanks by sharp practice. One evening God informed the dove that if he came early in the morning he would paint his legs a beautiful red. The Green Magpie happened to overhear this remark and got up very early, and coming to God first asked him to paint his legs. So God painted his legs a brilliant red. When the dove came a little later there was only old colour left. That is why the red of a dove's legs is dull.

Hugh of St. Victor, reflecting upon the Church, had a harsher vision:

The dove has two wings even as the Christian has two ways of life, the active and the contemplative. The blue feathers of the wings are thoughts of heaven; the uncertain shades of the body, the changing colours that recall an unquiet sea, symbolise the ocean of human passion in which the Church is sailing. Why are the dove's eyes this beautiful golden colour? Because yellow, the colour of ripe fruit, is the colour too of experience and maturity, and the yellow eyes of the dove are the looks full of wisdom which the Church casts on the future. The dove, moreover, has red feet, for the Church moves through the world with her feet in the blood of the martyrs.[8]

Somewhere, hidden in the lineage of the dove and probably in that of most birds, is a silent gene for feathered legs. The ptarmigan, which burrows quietly under the snow, hunting for mosses, has made good use of it, for its feet are densely feathered. The captive pigeon living in cold cotes may also find it advantageous, and Picasso has immortalized this man-made revelation with an angel bird of amazing beauty. Its sanglant feet are totally concealed by sweeping plumes.

Innocence

21

The White Fantails

White as the whitest dove's unsullied breast.[1]

When Elena was four years old she told a visitor that the fallow deer in the park once came up and talked to her. What an imaginative little girl! but Elena knew, even as she said it, that this was an invention. The fallow deer were shy and distant creatures – you only saw their outline and then they raised their heads and lifted their tails and lightly and perversely walked away. You never saw their eyes. But Elena wanted their nearness so ardently that she told her fairy tale with conviction and delight, for she experienced the secure biophilic pleasure from the propinquity of animals or growing plants.[2]

A few years later she set about the apparently hopeless task of persuading the White Fantails that lived in a loft at the end of the garden to come to her barred bedroom window to be fed. A ponderous man with a chip basket full of maize appeared near the dovecote punctually at nine o'clock each morning and his melodious whistle and cry of come-come! brought Elena rushing to her window and the pigeons – dropping like giant shiny snowflakes from the slated roof – to feed on the corn he scattered for their breakfast. Elena surreptitiously saved all her crusts and stole the odd slice of bread, and this was laid out in neat rows on her sloping stone window-ledge – most unsuitable for a bird to perch upon – and 'come-come' she cried in a hopeful imitation of the man's melodious whistle, yet her voice sounded silly in her own ears. . . .

One day a single pigeon flew down on to the sloping stone window-ledge immediately below hers. It seemed to glance at the bread offering on her sill as it passed. Her heart stopped. She saw each feather in its outspread wings, its amazing whiteness and smooth outline. Then the bird gently glided down and settled on the lawn below. This was more than Elena could bear. She rushed along the passage to her mother's room. 'The pigeons!' she cried, 'they flew up to *my* window to feed. They fed out of *my* hand.' Her mother put her book aside. She was not herself a bird lover, but she sensed in the little girl's trembling excitement some of the intense emotion aroused in her. 'You know,' she said calmly, 'I thought in time you'd win them over,' and she put an arm round her to share her triumph.

Two days later the miracle really happened. Suddenly several of the

Pigeon child

But what is it sorrowing of?

Fantails dropped down from the roof-top and made a bold bid for the bread laid out on the sloping sill. They settled with a scramble and a great threshing of wings. Elena felt their feathers – surprisingly stiff and hard – brush against her hand. A wild joy seized her. She watched incredulously as they fought in nervous excitement for the bread, knocking most of it to the ground and sailing down like angels with outstretched wings to retrieve the prize.

'The pigeons!' she cried in ecstasy. 'The pigeons! They have been to my window – I felt their wings – oh, oh, they have *really* been to my window.'

In later years she could recall the sense of disillusionment – for how could she explain – as her mother looked up in mild surprise and with only perfunctory enthusiasm. 'I expect they will come every day now, you know – once they realise the bread is there. . . .'

The profound desire for friendship and identification with wild animals and the craving to touch them and to share their aliveness is eventually lost, but at the imprinting stage it is experienced with almost painful intensity. When the canary came from nowhere and settled on André Gide's shoulder – he was then aged five – in a dreary grey Paris street full of the sound of rumbling traffic, he felt he had been chosen by God. The White Fantails granted Elena that special happiness which, like a faint shadow or rustle of wings, never quite deserted her.[3]

'. . . as if the sound belonged to someone else'

22

When That Her Golden Couplets Are Disclos'd[1]

Some birds must learn how to sing their special songs by listening to their parents. But wood-pigeons, if they are reared in captivity, divorced from the outside world, and never hear the gentle cooing of their peers, suddenly burst forth one summer morning at 5 a.m. with the familiar sound and cadence. They 'Take-two-cows-taffy' without a model, without any practice, and without hesitation, with the right pause after 'Take' and the correct emphasis on 'two.' There is something profoundly moving and delightful when for the first time a young pigeon spontaneously, and with no apparent cue, says its piece, word and tone perfect, a link in an unbroken chain of gently bubbling sound which has emerged from beneath a canopy of green leaves, in early morning sunshine, for thousands of years. The pigeon itself always looks somewhat taken aback – as if the sound belonged to someone else.

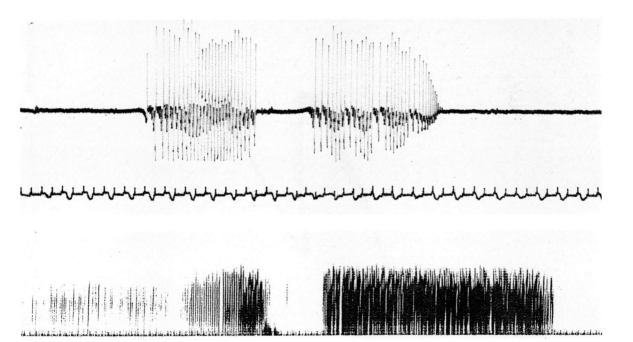

Sound traces

Matisse

23

Picasso and His Doves

Sit here, and see the turtle-dove,
Court his chaste mate to acts of love[1]

The pigeons cooed but the two turtle-doves really laughed. They were small and greyish-pink with a darker ruff around the neck. Every time we went into the kitchen to eat and Pablo launched into one of his characteristic long semi-philosophical monologues, the turtle-doves would be all attention. Just at the moment he made his point, they would start to laugh.

'These are really birds for a philosopher,' Pablo said. 'All human utterance has its stupid side. Fortunately I have the turtle-doves to make fun of me. Each time I think I'm saying something particularly intelligent, they remind me of the vanity of it all.'

Etruscan ceiling

The two turtle-doves were in the same cage and they often went through what seemed to be the act of mating but there was never any egg as a result. Finally Pablo decided there had been a mistake and they were both males.

'Everyone speaks so well of animals,' he said. 'Nature in its purest state and all that. What nonsense! Just look at these turtle-doves: as whole-heartedly pederast as two bad boys.'

He made two lithographs of them in action[2] . . .

Françoise Gilot

24

Mary and the Dove

> Thou from the first
> Wast present, and with mighty wings outspread
> Dovelike satst brooding on the vast abyss,
> And madest it pregnant.[1]

John 'bare record, saying, I saw the Spirit descending from heaven like a Dove, and it abode upon him.'[2] Mark, Matthew, and Luke shared the felicitous vision. There was no mistake – all four saw the Dove cleave the skies: 'white wings dripping ether bluer than air.'[3]

The mediaeval theologians preferred Luke's interpretation of the Immaculate Conception, and envisaged Mary 'over-shadowed' by the Holy Ghost; thus 'the bodily shape of a bird' appears in many great pictures portraying the annunciation. El Greco caught the wild incandescent beauty of the dove – sometimes tinged with terror – as no one else, but Crivelli was better acquainted with homely pigeons in their cotes, and shows us a plump feathered friend, with a trim but generous halo, slipping down a gilded shaft on matter-of-fact wings, carrying those most improbable tidings. Meanwhile, the rest of the flock, with insouciance and grace, go about their amorous business near the roof-tops.

In the High Middle Ages certain rather unimaginative and possibly prudish clerics insisted that Mary conceived through her ear (*conceptio per aurem*). The dove, presumably, achieved fertilization indirectly, by means of whispered commands via the least carnal of the apertures, and Mary is usually shown meekly bowing her enchanting head in acceptance of God's strange plan.

In his 18th-century *Columbarium* Moore tells us that 'the false prophet Mohammed' saw great possibilities in training the dove. With a few hemp seeds partially concealed in the wax exudate within his ears, he 'imposed upon the ignorant Arabians' – who, seeing the bird attempt to find the hidden grain, only too readily believed that the dove was in the process of whispering Allah's sacred commands into his servant's ear. Centuries later a page, concealed behind a curtain in the Vatican, claimed that he watched Pope Gregory the Great's dove, which always perched upon his shoulder, cooing into his master's ear, obviously dictating his *magnum opus* to the saintly man.

. . . oaring down mid-air from Heaven

'Thirsty doves in a parliament of birds shiver with love'

It is strange that no great painter, or even a Salvador Dali, has made the Dove – so pointedly absent at the fatal hour – the central subject of the place of a skull.

> And though the last lights off the black West went
> Oh, Morning, at the brown brink eastward, springs –
> Because the Holy Ghost over the bent
> World broods with warm breast and with ah! bright wings.[4]

There, waiting to be painted, is the immense, snowy, buoyant super-dove – occupying most of the canvas – bathed in a fierce holy light, and far, far beneath in another world – like the small landscape vignettes so beloved of Dürer and Leonardo, a miniature, almost irrelevant rocky hilltop with its three pygmy crosses, black against a pale green Renaissance sky, and Mary, looking on afar off, weeping.

> Dove, the love and the spirit
> Which engendered Jesus Christ,
> Like you I love a Mary.
> May I marry her![5]

The immense, snowy, buoyant super-dove

25

Milk

Sounds can be wonderfully nostalgic, and I regret the musical swish of a thin stream of milk rhythmically hitting the bottom of the pail – something we are not likely to hear again in Britain. It was a unique and unforgettable sound, recalling early morning and high summer when the air is clear with a promise of great heat to come, the grave whispering dove[1] in the trees, and a hint of fragrant hay. Then there was the clink of that elongated metal dipper with the curled handle which hung on the side of the bucket as it swung on the scales. It was from this receptacle that my glass was filled and misted over, the creamy bubbles softing round the brim. Warm milk. Straight from the cow at 5 a.m., generously slopping over the top of the dipper – the most deliciously evocative drink in the world.

Today, in a modern unit, one does not so much as catch a glimpse of the milk. It leaves the cow by means of little rubber and metal suction pumps, which hiss onto each individual teat. It then flows on, cooled, through sterilized aluminium tubes, into a giant tanker which eventually rumbles off into the distance, with the Rolling Stones blaring from its cab; small wonder that it no longer tastes quite the same. . . .

It is a capricious trick of nature that the doves, the embodiment of the Holy Spirit, should have stolen a leaf from our earthy, mammalian book and provide milk for their young. Furthermore, the hormone prolactin, which is responsible for their analogous secretion, is shared with ourselves. This sets the heavenly birds apart from all the rest of their kind.

Pigeon's milk is produced in the walls of the crop, not the breast; it is formed by the wholesale degeneration of the cell structure of the outer layer. The solids contain 50 percent fat, but no sugar. No doubt in their flimsy, raft-like nests, the young birds need to be insulated against the cold by this preponderance of fat. It is significant that porpoises, which live in icy waters, have virtually solid milk (49 percent fat) also lacking sugar. Elephants, horses, and we ourselves have the sweetest milk.

The young chicks when they hatch are blind, naked but for a light, sparse golden down, and curiously feeble. They have no lips so they cannot suck – Bottom referred erroneously to any sucking dove – and their beaks, although soft, are rigid. The parent takes the bill into its own mouth and fills it with the semi-solid milk, somewhat resembling cottage cheese. As the nestlings grow stronger they are able to push down into the throat themselves, almost as far as the crop itself, and aspirate the secretions.

Both parents produce milk and share in feeding the young. The cock bird is so sensitive that if he is separated from the hen, he begins to lactate merely at the sight of her brooding. But most of the heavier injustices of love fall on her, since the female not only furnishes more milk but broods for 18 hours compared with her mate's six. At least he absolves her of responsibility during the sunniest part of the day, for he takes over the nest at 10 a.m. and leaves it again between 3 and 4 in the afternoon.

Male mammals of course do not secrete milk, but the females vary in their technique for feeding their offspring.

Whales, which suckle underwater, pump a jet of milk forcibly into their young, which hold the teat in the corner of their mouths but do not suck. This saves the baby whales from simultaneously imbibing a mouthful of sea water. Sea otters develop another strategy to cope with the water menace: the female floats high up on her back and the pups suck from the exposed nipples without difficulty. A number of birds – penguins, gulls, gannets, falcons and so forth – regurgitate semi-digested food for their young to feed on, but only the doves and pigeons produce, as we do, prolactin-engendered milk.

How much of this 'perfect food' does a parent bird secrete? This has not been ascertained accurately but there must be a copious supply, for the squabs double their weight during the first 48 hours of life, while it takes a human child one hundred and eighty days to do likewise. The parent birds provide this type of nourishment for only about 3 weeks, whereas some mammals suckle their young for months or even years.

Thus we have two parallel streams of milk production in the United Kingdom – the producers blissfully unconscious of one another. We possess a very large population of doves and pigeons – wood-pigeons alone number around five to six million breeding birds, all secreting milk at some period during spring and summer. Their numbers rise to about 10 million by the autumn. Quite apart from human milk production – a woman can produce up to 963 grammes per day and about 800,000 babies are born annually – we keep about ten and a half million head of cattle which provide us with over fifteen thousand million litres of milk per year.

There is little to connect these two vast streams of white fluid sweeping independently through our world – except the tenuous link that little birds have learned to uncap the bottles of cow's milk left on our door-steps, and steal cream from the top. In days gone by, before metal tubing replaced wooden mangers, it was claimed that if swallows abandoned their nests on the rafters, the cows gave bloody milk. But that was a long time since, and time has obliterated the meaning for us.

Death and resurrection

26

Rainbow Butterflies and Amorous Doves

> The butterfly counts not months but moments
> And has time enough[1]

Flicking through some of the quotations I had jotted down in the past, I was struck by the variety of adjectives, apart from the colours – the bronzes, crimsons, diamond-flaked, and leaf-gold – applied by poets to butterflies:

Simple butterfly (Petrarch)
Gilded butterfly (Shakespeare)
Angelic butterfly (Dante)
Religious butterfly (Levi)
Visionary butterfly (Browning)
Bewildered butterfly (Frost)
Joyous butterfly (Spenser)
Careless butterfly (Keats)
Downy butterfly (Cook)
Speckled butterfly (Aldrich)
Idle butterfly (Bryant and Proust)
Vain butterfly (Arnold)
Inquisitive butterfly (Nabokov)
Coy butterfly (Graves)
Dizzy butterfly (Smith)
Flaky butterfly (Macdonald)
Jewelled butterfly (Arnold)
Chaste butterfly (Balaguer)
Crystal butterfly (Góngora)
Obsidian butterfly (Nicholson)
Painted butterfly (Shakespeare)
Languid butterfly (Larcom)
Wild butterfly (Machado)
Freckled butterfly (Davies)
Silly butterfly (Bunyan)
Peerless butterfly (Pope)
Funereal butterfly (Ovid)
Elegant butterfly (Querido)

In the plural we can find pent-up, velvet, giddy, bright, desperate and rainbow butterflies. Yes, rainbow is acceptable, but why butterfly?

In his monumental tome *The Butterflies of New England*, Scudder writes, '. . . there is good reason to believe that the root meaning of the word [butterfly] dates back to early Egyptian history and as a hieroglyphic it is synonymous as representing the qualities of completeness and perfection which characterise the soul.'[2]

An English writer suggests the term is derived from better fly, or a yellow fly, therefore buttercup, therefore butterfly. Similarly the Germans call it *butterfleige* or *buttervogel* or *schmetterling*; the early Dutch, *botervlieghe* or *boterschijte*; and the Anglo Saxon, *butter-fleoge*. (Chaucer remarked that 'Swich talkying is not worth a boterflye.'[3]) The word for butterfly in Czech is *smetana*, in French *papillon*, in Spanish *mariposa*, in modern Greek *petalouda*, in Hungaria *pillango*, in Italian *farfalle*, and in Russian *babochka* ('little soul'), and, of course, in ancient Greek there was one word for both butterfly and soul – *psyche*.

> The butterfly the ancient Grecians made
> The Soul's fair emblem, and its only name –
> But of the Soul, escape the slavish trade
> Of mortal life! – For in the earthly frame
> Ours is the reptile's lot, much toil, much blame,
> Manifold motions making little speed,
> And to deform and kill the things whereon we feed.[4]

The Encyclopaedia of Traditional Symbols[5] considers that the butterfly is an emblem of soul, immortality, rebirth, resurrection. The Chinese likewise considered it a symbol of immortality, abundant leisure, and joy. Joined to a chrysanthemum it signalled beauty in old age and with plum blossom, longevity. The rainbow originated, so they claimed, from transformed butterflies.

Adjectives describing the dove are less numerous and less imaginative than those lavished by poets on the butterfly. Once you have disposed of the white and blue, silver and golden and burnished doves, you are left with a series of rather monotonous terms of sugary endearment. 'Darling dove' appears frequently and 'sweet' or 'sweetest dove' even more often. Then follow timid, feeble, trembling, tender, faithful, mild, laggard, startled, and wild dove. And again: grave, whispering, murmuring, amorous, wedded dove. Occasionally one finds a hungry or thirsty dove, and one or two curiosities turn up, like flake doves or sucking doves, and finally there is the Holy Dove.

Leda and the Swan

The butterflies dream of flowers. I fain would ask – But it is voiceless

Traditionally this heavenly bird symbolises the life spirit,[6] the soul, the passing from one state or world to another, the spirit of light, chastity, innocence, gentleness, peace. In China it symbolises longevity, faithfulness, orderliness, filial piety, and spring. *The Encyclopaedia of Traditional Symbols* adds that in Parsee it represents the Supreme Being and in Sumero-Semitic, divine power.

Man's attitude, however, has always been rather ambivalent towards the animals he loved and worshipped.

Thus the bird of peace was, in Japan, sacred to Hachiman, the God of War, although, with a sword, it signified the end of war. For the ancient Hebrews the dove embodied the soul of the dead, yet their altars streamed with the blood of these birds, which were sacrificed as offerings of purity to God. The same ambivalence is seen where moral qualities are concerned.

A Butterfly meeting

Thus, the Chinese equated doves with both faithfulness and lasciviousness, while in Japan a pair of butterflies symbolised conjugal happiness, yet this insect also represented a vain woman, a geisha and a fickle lover. In ancient Mexico butterflies were worshipped as gods of beauty and love, and they also accompanied the Fire Goddess onto the battlefields. In Celtic literature they represent both the soul and fire.

A subtly less serious mood is apparent in folklore and local myths. Red butterflies are witches; the red meat of the dove is an aphrodisiac, and, placed above the house door, their entrails will attract back a roving lover.

Dividing the evening

An Irish myth declares that on returning to the Ark in obedience to Noah, the dove received the raven's sheen. The devil can take any shape but not that of a dove or a lamb, and finally no-one can die on a pillow stuffed with doves' feathers, since the bird symbolises the Holy Ghost and death cannot strike in His presence.

In the *Book of Odes*[7] attention is drawn to a peculiar couplet:

> The Turtle Dove is in the Mulberry Tree,
> And her young ones are seven in number

This accords well with the belief that in all religions of antiquity, the number seven is a sacred number. There were, as we know, seven attributes of the Holy Spirit and on the seventh day God rested. . . . The ancient Egyptians tabled seven mortal sins and the Babylonians seven wicked spirits. Somewhere, I feel, there must be a myth which reveals how and why the dove's clutch of seven eggs was reduced to two, but so far I have failed to discover it.*

As we have seen, the poets are more enthralled by the dove's beautiful flight than either its virtues or its shivering purity.

*But see Dähnhardt *Natursagen III*, 27, Helsinki 1964.

Comme elle fût belle parfois, la vie
Pendant que durait un vol de palombe †[8]

The ancient Egyptians, in an attempt to paint the lily, attached hollow reeds of different lengths to their tame pigeons' tail feathers, which then produced a pleasant musical sound as the birds flew around.

The sense of terror and futility engendered by shooting the pigeons 'borne on liquid wings'[9] is well described by Iris Murdoch:

> Through tears I saw the stricken birds tumbling over and over down the sloping roofs of warehouses. I saw and heard their sudden weight, their pitiful surrender to gravity. How harrowing to the heart it must be to do this thing: to change an innocent soaring being into a bundle of struggling rags and pain.[10]

Milton is wonderfully eloquent with his 'turtle wings the amorous clouds dividing,'[11] and Montgomery with the dove which 'on silver pinions winged her peaceful way'[12] catches the bird as she flies to her roost, remote and unaware of the significance of the spires of Oxford spread beneath her, or the grim huddle of the London suburbs.

The line I like the best is Salvatore Quasimodo's

> the sudden flapping of doves that divided the evening[13]

It reminds me of the way sound travels when a fine summer afternoon draws to a close – you remember the wheels creaking as the hay carts trundle home, and clear voices carry across the fields which would have been lost in the daze of mid-afternoon July sunshine. And suddenly, against the pale jade sky, there is a clap of wood-pigeons' wings.

† How beautiful life can sometimes be while a flight of pigeons is sustained.

27

Valley of the Butterflies

He seeks his hope in thee
Of immortality[1]

The moth which catches the eye of artists, from the Dutch still-life masters to the designers of twentieth-century posters, is distinguished by a nine-syllable name in Latin, and in Greek by a misnomer – for in Rhodes today it is known as a butterfly not a moth.

The unique assemblage of these insects was already a matter of interest in antiquity, for a Roman coin struck on the island has a moth or butterfly engraved on its upper surface.

In the third week of May the Jersey Tigers begin to assemble in their thousands in the Valley of the Butterflies, which is a deep cleft in a rocky hillside shadowed over by a forest of closely set plane trees. A stream cascades down the rocks into the floor of the valley where it slows down and forms a clear, gentle, shallow rivulet. The valley is deliciously cool and dark and silent, lit by green sunlight penetrating through the dense cover of leaves. One by one the Tigers flicker in, settling on the wet rocks and the trunks of the plane trees alongside the stream. They have bright, brick-red hindwings and black forewings streaked with pale yellow lines. Most of them sit in a neat triangle with their hindwings concealed, but here and there one shows a flash of scarlet. Gradually the rocks round the waterfall and the larger tree trunks become closely packed with moths. Now and again one or two shift off the damp moss and fly through the spray flung off the edge of the waterfall cascading into the pool below, and then settle again quietly on the crowded surface.

If a bird whistles near by, or a field mouse utters a supersonic squeak, the whole concourse rise into the air in their thousands and whirl round for a moment and then sink down again like a flurry of autumn leaves.

One or two specimens, at this period of the year, have been sacrificed to satisfy the curiosity of entomologists, who have demonstrated that their bodies are packed with fat reserves. Providing the moths are protected from the sun's penetrating rays, they have enough food stored to last them during the summer months – dreaming away the heat of the day on the wet rocks, but rising in unison at nightfall to the crown of the plane trees, where they quietly bask in the moonlight sitting motionless on the surface of the leaves.

The sheep and the Red Admiral

At sunrise, when the first oblique rays touch the tops of the trees, as if by some magic signal the moths fall into the bed of the valley below, floating down like scarlet and yellow autumn leaves in a windless dawn, to resume their mass slumber on the damp surface of the rocks.

In September when the ivy is in full bloom and the ling on the edge of the valley is sprayed with purple flowers, a change of mood is engendered in the thousands of aestivating moths. After dark, high up in the crown of the plane trees, a sexual orgy takes place.

Let copulation thrive . . .[2]

At dawn a few pairs cannot separate and fall to the ground in a deathly coitus, some landing in the water, still clasped together as the stream washes over them. Accidentally released – by a kindly human hand – from this fatal marriage bed, the moths fly away, apparently none the worse for their strange experience. Clearly, the wings of a species which deliberately flies in and out of a waterfall must be especially protected against wetting!

The moths are now no longer bound to the shady floor of the valley. They can be seen in their hundreds bejewelling the ivy blossom and the flowers of the ling in the sunshine along the edge of the valley. Again a few specimens, sacrificed on the dubious altar of science, were shown to contain depleted fat bodies and developing eggs. It could also be demonstrated by counting the number of spermatophores present in their reproductive ducts that they have been successfully impregnated, not once but on several occasions. A more sophisticated investigation revealed that these moths were not warningly coloured for nothing: they contained an array of defensive chemicals and emitted, into the bargain, a strong warning scent of pyrazine – the aromatic substance they share with, among others, the Monarch butterfly.

The sights and sounds of the Valley of the Butterflies are indelibly fixed in my mind. The cool, dark green sunlight, the host of silent moths dreaming away the summer months in their coordinated thousands, responding instantly to the whistle of a bird or the supersonic whisper of a field vole. Is it the scent of the pyrazines that has mysteriously imprinted the scene so vividly on my senses? Perhaps we will be able to harness this elusive perfume to evoke clear memories of the past and provide a retrieval mechanism which will unlock the store of long-forgotten events and emotions.

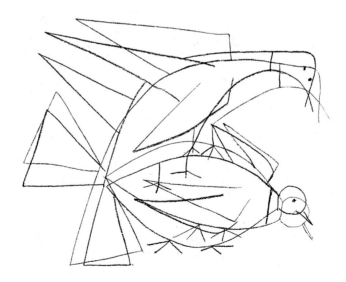

28

Brodsky's Butterfly and Gittings' Great Moth

The Great Moth

Visitant to our humbly human home,
Dull coal or shrivelled leaf, the great moth lay,
Out of storm-wet October came,
The window's lashing spray.

Strange confidant, the legs that crooked my finger
Settled like truth, though little I had to give,
Knowing how short such breath-spans linger,
How brief the creatures live.

Yet wishing to offer the slightest goodwill gesture,
Placed with free hand a bowl of honeysuckle near,
And sudden as a charm, the charred vesture
Was shed: a tremble like a tear

Shook the rose-barred body and vibrant wings,
Delight stood quivering in violent, delicate spread.
Above the sweetly-scented springs
Of life, it arose from the dead

Triumphant: and not one of us, bending over,
But felt the catch of hope and courage of heart,
As if with plumes of grace to hover
A spirit took our part.

Robert Gittings

The Butterfly

I

Should I say that you're dead?
You touched so brief a fragment
of time. There's much that's sad in
the joke God played.
I scarcely comprehend
the words 'you've lived'; the date of
your birth and when you faded
in my cupped hand
are one, and not two dates.
Thus calculated,
your term is, simply stated,
less than a day.

II

It's clear that days for us
are nothings, zeros.
They can't be pinned down near us
to feed our eyes.
Whenever days stand stark
against white borders,
since they possess no bodies
they leave no mark.
They are like you. That is,
each butterfly's small plumage
is one day's shrunken image –
a tenth its size.

III

Should I say that, somehow,
you lack all being?
What, then, are my hands feeling
that's so like you?
Such colours can't be drawn
from nonexistence.
Tell me, at whose insistence
were yours laid on?
Since I'm a mumbling heap
of words, not pigments,

how could your hues be figments
of my conceit?

IV

There are, on your small wings,
black spots and splashes –
like eyes, birds, girls, eyelashes.
But of what things
are you the airy norm?
What bits of faces,
what broken times and places
shine through your form?
As for your *nature mortes*:
do they show dishes
of fruits and flowers, or fishes
displayed on boards?

V

Perhaps a landscape smokes
among your ashes,
and with thick reading glasses
I'll scan its slopes –
its beaches, dancers, nymphs.
Is it as bright as
the day, or dark as night is?
And could one glimpse –
ascending that sky's screen –
some blazing lantern?
And tell me, please, what pattern
inspired this scene?

VI

It seems to me you are
a protean creature,
whose markings mask a feature
of face, or stone, or star.
Who was the jeweller,
brow uncontracted,
who from our world extracted
your miniature –

a world where madness brings
us low, and lower,
where we are things, while you are
the thought of things?

VII

Why were these lovely shapes
and colours given
for your one day of life in
this land of lakes?
– a land whose dappled mirrors
have one merit:
reflecting space, they store it.
Such brief existence tore
away your chance
to be captured, delivered,
within cupped hands to quiver –
the hunter's eye entrance.

VIII

You shun every response –
but not from shyness
or wickedness or slyness,
and not because
you're dead. Dead or alive,
to God's least creature
is given voice for speech, or
for song – a sign
that it has found a way
to bind together,
and stretch life's limits, whether
an hour or day.

IX

But you lack even this:
the means to utter
a word. Yet, probe the matter;
it's better thus.
You're not in heaven's debt,
on heaven's ledger.

It's not a curse, I pledge you,
that your small weight
and span rob you of tongue.
Sound's burden, too, is grievous.
And you're more speechless,
less fleshed, than time.

                    X
Living too brief an hour
for fear or trembling,
you spin, motelike, ascending
above this bed of flowers,
beyond the prison space
where past and future
combine to break, or batter,
our lives, and thus
when your path leads you far
to open meadows,
your pulsing wings bring shadows
and shapes to air.

                    XI
So, too, the sliding pen
which inks a surface
has no sense of the purpose
of any line
or that the whole will end
as an amalgam
of heresy and wisdom;
it therefore trusts the hand
whose silent speech incites
fingers to throbbing –
whose spasm reaps no pollen,
but eases hearts.

                    XII
Such beauty, set beside
so brief a season,
suggests to our stunned reason
this bleak surmise:

the world was made to hold
no end or *telos*,
and if – as some would tell us –
there is a goal,
it's not ourselves.
No butterfly collector
can trap light or detect where
the darkness dwells.

XIII

Should I bid you farewell
as to a day that's over?
Men's memories may wither,
grow thin, and fall
like hair. The trouble is,
behind their backs are:
not double beds for lovers,
hard sleep, the past,
or days in shrinking files
backstretched – but, rather,
huge clouds, circling together,
of butterflies.

XIV

You're better than No-thing.
That is, you're nearer,
more reachable, and clearer.
Yet you're akin
to nothingness –
like it, you're wholly empty.
And if, in your life's venture,
No-thing takes flesh,
that flesh will die.
Yet while you live you offer
a frail and shifting buffer,
dividing it from me.

Joseph Brodsky
1973/Translated by George L. Kline

29

Dreams

Dreams empty dreams. The million flit as gay
  As if created only like the fly,
That spreads his motley wings in the'ye of noon[1]

Moths and butterflies and dreams are deliciously confused – some nocturnal
blackness, mothy and warm:[2]

 . . . at mothy curfew tide,
And at midnight when the noon heat breathes
    it back from walls and leads,
They've a way of whispering. . . .[3]

And an agreeable dusting with stars and lost meteors, and watery reflections and a 'wing to brush as a half existent moth might on mere moonlight'[4]

Ilex and yew and dream enticing dark,
Hid pools; moths; creeping odours, stillness.
Luna its deity and its watchword Hark!
A still and starry mystery where in move
Phantoms of ageless wonder and of love.[5]

*

The moths came out, the swift grey moths of the dusk, that only visit
flowers for a second, never settling but hanging an inch or two above
the yellow of the Evening Primrose, vibrating to a blur. . . .[6]

And then suddenly it is night.
      . . . like stars
Moths fall into a mounting shaft of light.[7]

And

In time like glass the stars are set,
And seeming-fluttering butterflies
Are fixed fast in Time's glass net
With mountains and with maids' bright eyes.[8]

Confused, muddled, day, night, breathless, unreal.

Fairyland; silk-beech, scrolled ash, packed sycamore, wild wychelm,
hornbeam fretty overstood
By. Rafts and rafts of flake leaves light, dealt so, painted on the air,
Hang as still as hawk or hawkmoth, as the stars or as the Angels there. . . .[9]

And then Samuel Palmer ties up the stars:

We are like the chrysalis asleep and dreaming of its wings[10]

I know of no entomologist or ornithologist worth his salt who has not seen a rare or desirable or fantastic new species of bird or butterfly in his dreams. Usually such specimens are beautiful, brightly coloured, discovered in flowering landscape or an enchanting sunny woodland glade. These are straightforward, wish-fulfilment dreams, and there is no need to interpret them. No-one in his right mind could suggest that these successful butterfly hunts are metaphorical, or a disguise for subconscious, unacceptable wishes or desires.

But should we apply the kind of interpretation usually reserved for dreams to diurnal reality? We begin to wonder. . . . What are we *really* after when we set out with our green net, our pill boxes and our field-glasses? Are we chasing lost memories of prehistoric hunting adventures, scientific information, or childhood fantasies or mature desire and dreams? What do butterflies and birds really signify for us? What is the hidden symbolism extending from the morning chase to our night life?

I once met a heroic lady who had distinguished herself in the French resistance in World War II. Captured and tortured by the Gestapo, she had not given away a single name or revealed a single secret. She asked me if, during the day, I was influenced or disturbed by my dreams of the previous night. No, of course I wasn't – I forgot them or disregarded them immediately. She agreed that she did too. But in her case the events of the day had no more importance or meaning for her than the happenings of the night. Just as the act of waking dismissed her dreams, so at bedtime the slate was wiped clean and the events of the last 12 hours became as insignificant as those of the previous night, or the one that lay ahead.

He does not need to reveal by his dreams the archetypal layers of the psyche

It is, in a way, reminiscent of the musings of the Chinese poet:

> I dreamt, and in my dream
> I was a butterfly.
> I woke; or is it simply
> That, weary of the sky,
> Some butterfly is sleeping
> And dreams that it is I?[11]

Perhaps this fusing of night and day – a rather negative if consoling state of affairs for my heroine of the French resistance – is well illustrated by the dedicated and enthralled naturalist. He does not need to reveal by his dreams the archetypal layers of the psyche – they are there in broad daylight for everyone to see and envy.

What are we really hunting with our nets and pill boxes?

Nay, if you come to that, Sir, have not the wisest of man in all ages, not excepting Solomon himself – have they not had their HOBBY-HORSE – their running horses, their coins, and their cockleshells, their drums and trumpets, their fiddles, their pallets – their maggots and their butterflies?

A bird did 'hunt the jewelled butterfly'

30

Disasters

> . . . We pinned Jesus
> Like a lovely butterfly against the wood[1]

The disasters in the butterfly world attract less attention than those which befall doves or pigeons. Poets write about butterflies drowning in ink-wells, or smashed on the windscreens of motor cars. (Pope, who asked, 'Who breaks a butterfly upon a wheel?'[2] did not know about charabancs and lorries.) And these insects are for ever snapped up by hungry birds.

> The bulbul which did hunt
> The jewelled butterfly . . .[3]

Incidentally, Arnold was an observant naturalist, as well as a great poet, since the bulbul is one of the few avian species which can eat brightly coloured toxic butterflies with impunity.

The fact that the dove is a sweet, defenceless, faithful creature, living apparently in a state of perpetual anxiety, touched the hearts of many poets.

Keats wrote, . . . 'poor ring doves sleek forth their timid necks and tremble . . .[4]

While Virgil describes their fright when a sea-race is in progress.

> The Crew of Mnestheus, with elated Minds,
> Urge their Success, and call the willing Winds:
> Then ply their Oars, and cut their liquid way;
> In larger Compass on the roomy Sea.
> As when the Dove her Rocky Hold forsakes,
> Rouz'd in a Fright, her sounding Wings she shakes:
> And leaves her Callow Care, and cleaves the Skies;
> At first she flutters; but at length she springs,
> To smoother flight, and shoots upon her Wings . . .[5]

Edmund Spenser muses in a gentler frame of mind, but the dove is still suffering:

> The Turtle on the bared branch,
> Laments the wound that death did launch . . .[6]

And death is always present in the guise of an eagle:

> Not half so swift the trembling Doves can fly,
> When the fierce Eagle cleaves the liquid sky[7]

and again:

> Shattered and torn before the flag they fly,
> Like doves that the exalted eagle spy.[8]

and:

> Over the laggard dove, inclinging to green boscage,
> Hovers the intentional doom – till the unsullied sky receives
> A precipitation of shed feathers
> And the swifter fall of wounded wings.[9]

In the temple wall in Jerusalem (the tourists' so-called Wailing Wall) both doves and hawks nest and live amicably in the holes and crevices, and must have done so since the days of Solomon. The kestrels, I imagine, are only interested in smaller prey the size of sparrows or mice, for I have never seen one of them so much as glance with interest at the insouciant doves. In mediaeval times in the falconer's hierarchy the only bird of prey a knave

The fierce eagle cleaves the liquid skies

or servant could own was a kestrel – we can conclude it was not a great
performer. (There was only one lower category – the sparrow-hawk for
the clergy.)

Of course, mankind has destroyed more pigeons than all the eagles and
long-winged hawks put together. The passenger-pigeon, a colonial nester,
was, for instance exterminated within living memory in North America.
Millions of these beautiful birds bred in fatally huge accessible congrega-
tions, and were readily available for mass slaughter.

Audubon thus described the migration of these birds:

The air was literally filled with Pigeons; the light of noon-day was
obscured as by an eclipse; the dung fell in spots, not unlike melting
flakes of snow. The Pigeons were still passing in undiminished numbers,
and continued to do so for three days in succession.[10]

And then an endless bloody stream flowed to the altars in Egypt and Israel, although some of these birds must have been bred in captivity to keep up with the ceaseless demand.

> Look in the literature [says Bernard Lazare], there is no bird so persecuted as the Dove: nevertheless it was she that God chose to be sacrificed on his altar. God said: 'Offer me in holocaust not those who persecute but those who are persecuted.'[11]

In the Third Book of Moses we are given explicit instruction about the sacrifice of turtle doves and young pigeons (old pigeons were not acceptable).

> And the priest shall bring it unto the altar, and wring off his head, and burn it on the altar; and the blood thereof shall be wrung out at the side of the altar: And he shall pluck away his crop with his feathers, and cast it beside the altar on the east part, by the place of the ashes: And he shall cleave it with the wings thereof, but shall not divide it asunder: and the priest shall burn it upon the altar, upon the wood that is upon the fire: it is a burnt sacrifice, an offering made by fire, of a sweet savour unto the Lord.[12]

Mary and Joseph, it will be remembered, sacrificed a pair of turtle-doves or two young pigeons in Jerusalem, when the days of her purification were accomplished, and Jesus was circumcised and named.[13]

All in all, it seems rather odd that the dove was chosen as the symbol of the Holy Spirit.

*

Neither did 17th-century medicine spare the dove. When John Donne was seriously ill, the King's physician was sent to his bedside and prescribed the fashionable remedy of applying pigeons cut in half 'to draw the vapours from the Head.'[14] Pepys in his diary records that the Queen 'was so ill as to be shaved, and pigeons put to her feet.'[15]

The birds' melancholy voice, as we know, caught the imagination of the poets. Isaiah declared, we mourn sore like doves,[16] and Tennyson 'heard the tender dove in firry woodlands making moan.'[17] A modern poet, Stevie Smith, matches my own feelings about wood-pigeons. I spent about eighteen months of the Second World War studying their habits (as an employee of the Ministry of Agriculture) and got to know them well — independent, resourceful, and delightfully noisy birds, which kindle the affections.

The Old Sweet Dove of Wiveton

'Twas the voice of the sweet dove
I heard him move
I heard him cry
Love, love.

High in the chestnut tree
Is the nest of the old dove
And there he sits solitary
Crying, Love, love.

The grey of this heavy day
Makes the green of the trees' leaves and the grass brighter
And the flowers of the chestnut tree whiter
And whiter the flowers of the high cow-parsley

So still is the air
So heavy the sky
You can hear the splash
Of the water falling from the green grass
As Red and Honey push by,
The old dogs,
Gone away, gone hunting by the marsh bogs.

Happy the retriever dogs in their pursuit
Happy in bog-mud the busy foot.

Now all is silent, it is silent again
In the sombre day and the beginning soft rain
It is a silence made more actual
By the moan from the high tree that is occasional

Where in his nest above
Still sits the old dove,
Murmuring solitary
Crying for pain,
Crying most melancholy
Again and again.[18]

But to return to the butterflies:

Any species of bird or insect which congregates in huge numbers exposes itself to sudden disaster on a grand scale. For instance, the Monarch butterfly migrates southwards in the autumn, to winter in specific mountainous areas in the forests of Mexico.

> The monarch butterfly and his gliding brood
> Have gone. . . .[19]

These butterflies arrive there in their millions after a long, dangerous, and arduous flight, some flying in from as far north as Canada. It has been estimated that 10 to 12 million butterflies winter in a hectare of forest. One or two species of birds which are relatively unaffected by the poisonous contents of these insects' body tissues flock to the district and consume, during the winter, about 9 percent of these butterflies! Mice eat another 6 percent. It is a melancholy thought that thousands of freshly emerged butterflies fly dangerously and purposefully southwards, to a tryst with death. There must be a strange sort of safety in numbers – some unseen benefit accruing to the species as a whole – or this extraordinary life-style could not have been evolved and maintained.

*

Usually we are concerned with obscure little domestic tragedies:

> The swallows nested in the drawing room; the floor was strewn with straw; the plaster fell in shovelfuls; rafters were laid bare; rats carried off this or that to gnaw behind the wainscots. Tortoise-shell butterflies burst from the chrysalis and pattered their life out on the window pane.[20]

> A moth drowned in my urine
> his powdered body finally satin.
> My eyes gleamed in the porcelain
> like tiny dancing crematoria.

> History is on my side, I pleaded
> As the drain drew circles in his wings.
> (Had he not been bathed in urine
> I'd have rescued him to dry in the wind.)[21]

Lorca, possessed by 'a deaf and dumb weary exhaustion'[22] drowned his butterfly in an ink-well. 'What hand,' asked Shelley, 'would crush the silken-wingéd fly?'[23]

Small copper

Then there are the bitter personal disasters.

It is painful to write about not loving. I loved you to distraction, to the exclusion of every other thought . . . even when I was asleep I was consciously in love with you. I shrink from this new knowledge, said Ian, but I now know in my heart – although it is something difficult to bear – that you are a deeply destructive woman, despite your fearless, flame-like quality and your sudden tender, crumpled rose-petal smile. You have destroyed my ability to doze, you seem to have spread a film of mustard between me and the world, and you have dulled my fondness for butterflies – even for small coppers.[24]

'For over there is a dark chamber,' cried Pablo Neruda, 'with a broken candelabra. A few twisted chairs waiting for winter. And a dead dove with a number.'[25]

Finally both Victor Hugo and Erich Maria Remarque place their butterflies – albeit in different centuries – on the same giant canvas, fluttering carelessly on the bloody ramparts of the battlefield.

One morning two butterflies play in front of our trench. They are brimstone-butterflies, with red spots on their yellow wings. What can they be looking for here? There is not a plant nor a flower for miles. They settle on the teeth of a skull. . . .[26]

Summer, wrote Victor Hugo, does not abdicate:

There were a few corpses here and there and pools of blood on the pavement. I remember a white butterfly which came and went in the street[27] . . .

The butterfly hunt

31

Migration

> They shall tremble as a bird out of Egypt,
> and as a dove out of the land of Assyria.[1]

Shy doves, Moero tells us, fed Zeus with Ambrosia, drawn from the ocean, and out of gratitude he set them in the firmament as his starry Pleiades – to shine for ever and to make a sign to herald summer and the year's decline.[2] But other species of birds, ducks, and robins and warblers, which migrate at night, navigate by star pictures, for they can remember the position of a thousand stars. Pigeons migrate by day and navigate by the sun, and only on very rare occasions – which are disclosed when they are caught in the dangerous beam of a lighthouse – fly after sunset, for they usually rest during the hours of darkness. However, in World War I the United States Army trained homing pigeons to fly by night, when they were less molested by birds of prey. But how they found their way under moonless, overcast skies we do not know. On their autumn migration southwards from their breeding grounds to winter quarters, wild pigeons usually fly at great heights, three to six thousand feet above the ground. How long it takes them to reach their destination is not recorded either, but the birds stop periodically for feeding and resting. A trained racing pigeon in first-class condition can fly at a rate of 30 to 70 miles per hour – not so fast as some ducks and hawks or the chimney swift, but nevertheless at great speed. Furthermore, they can fly from the point of release to their home loft, set at a distance of five hundred to six hundred miles, within a day. This feat may be less impressive than that of the Laysan albatross, which homed from a distance of 6,629 km. in 12 days, or the 16,000 km. interpolar migration of the Arctic tern.

Pigeons find their way by a variety of cues, mostly visual cues. They recognise landmarks, woodlands, hills, highways, rivers, coastlines. They can store these mental pictures for months, even years. They not only navigate by the sun, but they can assess wind (and allow for it when they are swept off course) and appreciate the direction of the waves in the wrinkled sea crawling beneath them.[3] Experiments with tiny portable magnets attached to their heads have shown that the earth's magnetic field can provide them with directional information. It remains a mystery how the birds perceive these lines of force, but one expert has suggested that the magnetic

. . . Wavers the butterfly, ever across its path a pilot invisible leads . . .

field could alter molecules or atoms in sensory cells in a similar way to the molecular alteration by light in photoreceptors.[4]

It is also possible that pigeons travelling across the sea can, in anti-cyclonic weather, when it is fine and clear, pick up the different colours and shadows in the water resulting from the topography of the sea bottom, where black rocks and banks of olive green seaweed and gently heaving wrack are discerned as purple and indigo or brown patches of light or shade. Can they pick their way from the air along valleys in the seabed, in the same way that they can follow a coastline?

> Where thou perhaps under the whelming tide
> Visit'st the bottom of the monstrous world.[5]

What sort of spatial memory does a pigeon possess? What is its potential? What built-in clocks and endogenous temporal programmes do they respond to? We do not know. How for instance can the juvenile dove, migrating southwards on its first winter journey, without its parents or other experienced birds, know where to stop? How does the wandering albatross, which circumnavigates the South Pole, travelling with the prevailing westerly winds and returning unerringly to its home every year (this bird can live for half a century) know when the huge circle has been completed?

Drive on, sharp wings, and cry above
Not contemplating life or love,
Or war or death: a winter flight
Impartial to our human plight.

I below shall still remain
On solid earth, with fear and pain –
Doubt, and act, and nervous strive,
As best I may, to keep alive.

What useless dream, a hope to sail
Down the wide, transparent gale,
Until, insentient, I shall be
As gaseous a transparency.

What useless dream, a hope to wring
Comfort from a migrant wing:
Human or beast, between us set
The incommunicable net.

Parallel, yet separate,
The languages we mistranslate,
And knowledge seems no less absurd
If of a mistress, or a bird.[6]

*

Pliny tells us that pigeons acted as messengers in affairs of importance.[7] During the siege of Mutina, Decimus Brutus set dispatches to the camp of the consuls, fastened to pigeons' feet. Of what use to Antony then, he asks, were his entrenchments and all the vigilance of the besieging army . . . while the messenger of the besieged was cleaving the air?

163

There are very few early records of the pigeons' ability to 'home,' but it is believed that this knowledge was widespread among all the ancient civilisations. King Solomon (about 900 - 1000 B.C.) and Cyrus the Great of Persia (529 B.C.) are both reputed to have used these birds extensively to communicate within their kingdoms. In Greece the message-bearing pigeons were linked with the Oracles, and Strabo describes the two black doves which flew from Thebes in Egypt to Dodona to the Oracle of Zeus.[8] An extensive grove of trees was planted round Jupiter's Temple, where he claimed oracles were delivered by the sacred oaks and the doves that haunted their branches.

It was said that Taurosthenes stained a pigeon bright purple and released it, thus announcing his victory at the Olympic Games to his father. This set the fashion and thereafter many victors followed his example, and sent dyed birds to convey the good news to their families waiting anxiously at home.

There is something profoundly nauseating in man's misuse of animals in war – horses forced to charge blazing cannons, and shot to pieces as they galloped forward, or whales blown to bits by the explosive charges they were trained to carry into enemy harbours. They are forced to join us in our self-inflicted horror. Pigeons were likewise our victims, and without a moment of remorse or a flicker of doubt these birds were sent through a hail of bullets and gunfire, carrying messages to some distant headquarters. Levi[9] describes how, in the siege of Paris, dispatches were inserted in a small goose quill and tied by waxed silken thread to the strongest feather of the tail. With the aid of micro-photography it was possible to send twenty-five hundred messages in one tiny canister and 12 canisters per bird. On one occasion a single homer delivered forty thousand messages. During the occupation of Belgium in the 1914 war, the Germans confiscated over a million pigeons. It is not known how many were used by the combatants, but some idea of the numbers involved can be gauged by the fact that a monument at Lille in France was erected to commemorate the twenty thousand birds killed in action.

There exist some enthusiastic descriptions of the 'heroism of the Homers.' Several pigeons released with messages 'were unable to get through the hell of shell and shrapnel and fell to the ground mortally wounded.' Only one bird, cynically named 'Cherè Ami,' arrived with the message that saved the members of the 'lost battalion' – with one leg utterly shattered, although the bullet which carried away his leg had also passed through his breast. The message hung 'by a few shreds of sinew.'[9]

Other birds were partially blinded, their heads gashed and necks torn,

La Grande Famille

their feet shot away. 'In spite of these wounds, the bird sorely tried, had gallantly reached his home loft' – this bird was 'the Mocker,' who actually survived for 20 years after shrapnel had carried away his left eye and laid bare his brains. His body was eventually stuffed, mounted, and put on display. It is scarcely possible to envisage a more perfect indictment of the human race.

*

In Sweden, wood-pigeons fly south and winter in Spain, but the climate in Britain is less severe and the majority of our birds elect to remain in England and do not migrate. Nevertheless there is always a slight but definite movement southwards within the British Isles. The birds seem to have a *latent* desire to migrate, and this is probably a feature of related species like the collared dove which suddenly, during the fifties, spread from the Balkans to north-western Europe and established itself successfully over the area including the U.K. There is no clue which could lead one to identify the trigger which initiates the exodus. This remains a mystery. Is there a subtle change in climate? Has the population suddenly increased enormously? Have food supplies waxed or waned? Why this year rather than last year? Does one bird go at random and another and another get caught up in the frenzy of sudden departure? We do not know.

A similar latent migration urge is found too in certain butterflies, probably in the Monarch, a New World species which occasionally makes a successful Atlantic crossing and turns up in Devonshire. This butterfly, as we have said, undertakes a great annual migration of 3,000 km. from summer quarters in North America to winter hibernation in Mexico, but within the last century has also migrated to Australia, Hawaii, and New Zealand and settled there, and to various islands such as the Canaries and the Galapagos, where hitherto it was unknown.

On the Monarchs' southward passage in sunny weather, they are on the wing from 7.30 a.m. until 5 p.m. Probably only about 4 hours are spent in active migration, in which time they cover about 120 km. After the butterflies have travelled some 1,500 km., the urgency seems to fade from their flight; their rate of progress is reduced and they adopt the tempo and style of the spring migration.

One autumn I was collecting snails at dusk by a shaded stream in Rock Creek Park, Washington, D.C., when a large flight of Monarchs on their way south flew in and settled down for the night in the lower branches of the trees. I found their arrival disturbing. I recalled the beautiful 16th-and 17th-century Chinese paintings of butterflies in which the large Papilios and Nymphalids are given rather sinister faces, with slightly protruding eyes and beak-like mouthparts. Until I stood in the midst of this vast company of Monarchs preparing to rest for the night, I had had little sympathy with this Chinese convention, but suddenly the orange-and-black butterflies appeared rather sinister, and I had the fleeting impression of a hostile crowd. Many years later I discovered that Monarchs secrete an aromatic substance, a pyrazine, which has a strange evocative quality – a warning-of-danger quality. I was certainly not aware of any scent at all on this occasion, but in retrospect I wonder if a faint odour of pyrazines accounted for my desire to leave the area of the roost, instead of watching the phenomenon spellbound – as indeed I would today. The Monarch, as a caterpillar, sequesters and stores heart poisons from its food plant which are then incorporated in its chrysalis and thence pass into the adult butterfly. These bitter-tasting toxic cardenolides protect them from attack by many birds, and the pyrazines – also obtained via the tissues of their food plant – function as an *aide-mémoire* for the predators. A whiff of this persistent smell reminds them instantly of their past *malaise*, and the pain experienced after swallowing a bit of Monarch prey, and they fly off. No doubt the Monarchs resting on migration are enveloped in a thin protective vapour of pyrazines.

One spring morning, motoring along the California coast, I encountered a crowd of these butterflies journeying northwards towards their summer feeding grounds. They were sailing along in bright sunshine against an azure sky, in graceful ease and timeless harmony.

> . . . Wavers the butterfly,
> Ever across its path a pilot invisible leads . . .[10]

More fortunate still, later in the same season, I found myself on a road verge in Texas, in the midst of the more dramatic southward migration. The butterflies were well spaced out but moving quickly and strongly across country, only about three or four feet above my head. They rose vertically to negotiate the face of a tall building that lay in their path and flew purposefully onwards, engendering a sense of urgency and empyreal destiny as they swept past, one after another, in a seemingly endless succession. Meanwhile, motor cars rattled along and huge lorries thundered down the highway on their various human errands – the two streams of travellers passing at right angles, oblivious of each other – the Monarchs going silently about their butterfly business, with several thousand years of evolution to drive them forward, to dream away the winter in an icy communal torpor.

A big migration such as this of either birds or butterflies is an awesome sight and arouses strange and unexpected emotions of wide-eyed astonishment and wonder. With the anonymous Greek poet,[11] there is a sense of melancholy, tinged with relief that over our graves the wild geese will hum.

Taking a Sunflower to Teacher

32

Sorrow

> . . . if I be left behind,
> A moth of peace, and he go to the war,
> The rites for which I love him are bereft me . . .[1]

There are only two great sorrows in the world – loss of love and loss of life.

> Theirs was the bitterness we know
> Because the clouds of hawthorn keep
> So short a state, and kisses go
> To Tombs unfathomably deep.[2]

The anthropologist Premack decided not to teach his chimpanzee the concept of mortality until he could be absolutely sure he would not inadvertently also acquaint him with the fear of death.

What passes through the avian mind we do not know. I remember at one time we kept a small flock of love-birds in our laboratory which belonged to a strictly monogamous species,* the female hooked on the male's song – each one with a delicately individual tune. One day an epidemic of coccidiosis swept through the aviary, leaving several distraught widows and widowers. It was with the greatest difficulty that we managed to persuade a bereft female to accept and pair with another male. It so happened that before the epidemic struck we had recorded the various male songs. One afternoon someone put on the tape recorder and played back a song from one of the males we had lost. Instantly the widow left her new mate and quietly perched beside the machine. We felt extremely embarrassed and not a little melancholy.

The poets have chosen the dove as an emblem of grief:

> So shuts the marigold her leaves
> At the departure of the sun;
> So from the honeysuckle sheaves
> The bee goes when the day is done:
> So sits the turtle when she is but one,
> And so all woe, as I since she is gone.[3]

* *Agapornis verseicollis*

Butterflies don't live in here, in the ghetto

The pigeons are for ever sorrowing 'while the stock dove breathes a melancholy murmur thro' the whole. . . .'[4]

> The ring dove, in the embowering ivy, yet
> Keeps up her love lament, and the owls flit
> Round the evening tower, and the young stars glance
> Between the quick bats in their twilight dance.[5]

But then once again the poets use the dove as a term of endearment. They forsake nature and echo their own doubts and sadness.

> Like a pure and immaculate white dove
> Woe is me! Thus suddenly to God you flew,
> Blest spirit, and left me sightless
> In this valley of dark misery.[6]

And Victor Hugo, with his gentle gloom. . . .

> All hope, child, is but a reed,
> God in his hands, holds our days, my dove,
> He divides them with his fatal spindle
> Then the thread breaks and our joy is ended
> Since in every cradle
> There germinates a grave.[7]

A more subtle and poignant poem by Padraic Colum links the gentleness of the pigeons with the listener's gentle grief:

> I heard in the night the pigeons
> Stirring within their nests:
> The wild pigeons' stir was tender,
> Like a child's hand at the breast.
> I cried 'O stir no more!
> (My breast was touched with tears)
> O pigeons, make no stir –
> A childless woman hears.'[8]

Sometimes, very rarely, it is the dove herself which arouses the poet's insight:

> Rou-cou spoke the dove,
> Like the sooth lord of sorrow,
> Of sooth love and sorrow,
> And a hail-bow, hail-bow,
> To this morrow.
>
> She lay upon the roof,
> A little wet of wing and woe,
> And she rou-ed there,
> Softly she piped among the suns
> And their ordinary glare,
>
> The sun of five, the sun of six,
> Their ordinariness,
> And the ordinariness of seven,
> Which she accepted,
> Like a fixed heaven,
>
> Not subject to change . . .
> Day's invisible beginner,

Despair

The lord of love and of sooth sorrow,
Lay on the roof
And made much within her.[9]

*

Nabokov thought of butterflies on his deathbed:

'A few days before he died,' wrote his son, 'there was a moment I remember with special clarity. During our penultimate farewell, after I had kissed his still-warm forehead – as I had done for years when saying goodnight or goodbye – tears suddenly welled in Father's eyes. I asked him why. He replied that a certain butterfly was already on the wing; and his eyes told me he no longer hoped that he would live to pursue it again. Nor would he ever visit that enchanted mountain valley on the far side of the lake.'[10]

But by and large, butterflies play a profoundly different role: they are symbols of resurrection and escape from sorrow and death.

I was walking across an open rocky space in the city of Jerusalem, looking at the wild cyclamen in full bloom beneath the boulders, admiring the way each rock seemed to coax a different shade of pink out of the flowers, when I suddenly drew in a sharp breath and stopped. For there, drawn clearly with a weak piece of orange chalk on a block of concrete, was a butterfly. It was a butterfly every Jew and Jewess knows by heart, the butterfly drawn by children in German death camps before they went to the gas chambers. Fifteen thousand children had been incarcerated in one particular camp; only a hundred survived. It is the emblem of escape from the greatest sorrow the world has ever known.

'Leave me,' wrote Heine. 'Love only the fluttering butterfly in the sunshine. Leave me and my sorrow.'[11]

'. . . in the clefts of the rocks, in the secret places of the stairs'

33

Love

Show'd like two silver doves that sit a billing[1]

Pliny considered that chastity was especially observed by female doves, which were monogamous for life, and that promiscuous intercourse was a thing quite unknown: by nature they were incapable of infidelity. John Donne insisted: 'we find no Bigamy in the Turtle.'[2]

This may well be true if doves live in the woods and fields, but cooped up in lofts or dovecots, mated hens are not infrequently won over by a single lusty cock. Similarly a mated cock may be collected by passing lesbian hens. Strangely enough, once a lesbian pair is well established, the bond is a powerful one, and they become deeply attached to each other. A tie which is more than physical, wrote one pigeon lover, exists between the two.[3] After occasional intercourse with a philanderous cock they return to their female mates, the only signs of their temporary infidelity are the fertile eggs they lay in due course.

Copulation between doves takes a graceful second, but an elaborate, almost continuous courtship precedes the fleeting moment of fertilization. The great French naturalist, Buffon, was struck by the fact that although satisfaction was so brief, this moment was being repeated a few minutes later by new desires with fresh approaches, equally sincere; an ever-enduring flame, a desire ever constant, and what is even better, the power of satisfying it incessantly ... the whole term of life employed in the service of love and the care of its fruits.[4] Propinquity plays a major role in the amorous affairs of pigeons and it is enough for the female to hear the cock cooing to lay her two white eggs. If there is mutual agreement to mate, the cock opens his beak and the hen places hers within his, and a long marital kiss follows. Young, inexperienced birds prolong the kiss for several minutes but older birds become a little more casual.

Give me thy billing kiss, that of the Dove,
A Kiss of Love[5]

It is the unselfconsciousness of love between doves and between butterflies that unites them and sets them apart, endowing them with a quality denied us. Only a fortunate few who could crystallise their observations and link them to a subtle phrase or a gifted pencil, have fleetingly caught the felicitous mood.

'Some birds have movements peculiar to the seasons,' wrote Gilbert White. 'Thus ring-doves though strong and rapid at other times, yet in the Spring hang about on the wing in a toying and playful manner.'[6] And Moore remarked: 'These birds have many pretty and whimsical gestures when they are salacious.'[7]

Góngora likens the singing of amorous doves to hoarse and distant drums.

Picasso drew his copulating pigeons many times – occasionally males with males – illustrated with miraculous insight and humour and a few thin lines, the pure and original spring of love.[8]

On the whole, doves are caught by the poets to express their own sentiments, for they are not deeply concerned with the natural world, and one and all are moved by the staunch, rather strange monogamy of these sweet birds.

> They see two doves alight on gentle wing
> And, from the lustiest myrtle, in the thrill
> Of passion, moaning soft laments to move
> Their hearers with the clarion-call of Love.[9]

> With time still the affection groweth
> In the faithful turtle dove[10]

> The Dove was there with her meek eye. . . .
> The wedded turtle dove, with her faithful heart[11]

> That ardent dovelike tenderness. . . .[12]

And then 'dove' becomes a term of endearment, and admiration, and of love:

> Behold, thou art fair, my love;
> Behold, thou art fair;
> thou hast doves' eyes[13]

and, even more telling:

> Thou hast doves' eyes within thy locks[14]

and the mournful Spanish poet, with a *cri de coeur*:

> But this pure and white dove, whose equal I think
> never lived in this world, she resounds very little
> in my frail style.[15]

177

A great contrast is found in the wonderfully rich, sentimental Victorians' –
first Browning:

> How say you? Let us, O my dove,
> Let us be unashamed of soul,
> As earth lies bare to heaven above.
> How is it under our control
> To love or not to love?[16]

and then Tennyson:

> There has fallen a splendid tear
> From the passion-flower at the gate,
> She is coming, my dove, my dear;
> She is coming, my life, my fate.
> The red rose cries, 'She is near, she is near'
> And the white rose weeps, 'She is late.'
> The larkspur listens, 'I hear, I hear,'
> And the lily whispers, 'I wait.'[17]

Victor Hugo is gloriously, romantically Latin, describing his young lovers
meeting in a garden at dusk:

> Limpid purity. Innocent hours, almost all alike. This kind of love is a
> collection of lily petals and doves' feathers.[18]

T. S. Eliot's bird is fraught with *angst*:

> The dove descending breaks the air
> With flame of incandescent terror
> Of which the tongues declare
> The one discharge from sin and error,
> The only hope, or else despair
>   Lies in the choice of pure or pure –
>   To be redeemed from fire by fire
> Who then devised the torment? Love.
> Love is the unfamiliar Name
> Behind the hands that wove
> The intolerable shirt of flame
>   Which human power cannot remove.
>   We only live, only suspire
> Consumed by either fire or fire.[19]

But Shakespeare touches upon the sense of never-ending fornication engendered by captive pigeons.

> *Paris to Helen:* He eats nothing but doves, love; and that breeds hot blood, and hot blood begets hot thoughts, and hot thoughts beget hot deeds, and hot deeds is love.[20]

*

The love life of butterflies and moths contrasts strangely with that of doves. After pairing, male and female remain joined – as if soldered together – for hours and sometimes days. There is often a nuptial flight, when she soars clumsily into the blue carrying the male with her. Not infrequently the genitalia fail to separate and they both die slowly in a deathly coitus. Conversely courtship is elaborate but brief, and scent plays a major role in their mutual attraction. The nocturnal moths can detect the whereabouts of their future mates by the perfumed chemical message delivered by a single molecule – a sensitivity beyond our imagination.

We know very little about butterflies' eyesight but there is no doubt that their sex drive is initially stimulated by the brilliant colour of their partner's wings and the flashes of ultra-violet that we cannot see. But in order to captivate and enravish the female, the male, during courtship, dusts her with minute aphrodisiacal scent particles, which are secreted by specialised scales and hairs distributed over his wings, or concentrated on extruseable brushes at the end of his abdomen. In related species this love dust is always characteristic and both the delicate perfume and structure of the particles are subtly different – a startling glimpse of the immense and astonishing variety found in nature.

The female cabbage white butterfly receives during coitus, in addition to sperm, a chemical messenger – a pheromone – which is duly extruded with her eggs at oviposition. This is one of the volatile substances that inhibit other butterflies from laying on the same plant, and thus depleting the food supply of her future caterpillars. In this fashion the male protects his offspring, but his interest ceases once the act of procreation is over. The male dove, as we have seen, in great contrast to the 'small gilded fly,' secretes crop milk with which he nourishes his young and takes turns with his female in brooding the eggs as well as the nestlings.

The Heliconids are a group of gaudy, fragile, neotropical butterflies – striped red and gold and blue and green on a black background – that feed

179

Sex brushes

on passion flowers and have bewitched the naturalists, for no fewer than two hundred papers have been published about their biology and structure during the last decade. The males display a sexual ardour rarely met with in the insect world. They are attracted – probably by some subtle odour – to the chrysalis of the unhatched female. And they sit and wait in deadly quiet for her to struggle free. She is then raped by the most active and strongest of the two or three attendant males. Not infrequently desire gets the better of them and they violate her – or attempt to do so – while she is still within her chrysalis.

It is of course physically impossible for a bird to violate a young female chick within the egg, and even the most disturbed pigeon would not attempt this unnatural act.

Love dust

Virginia Woolf described the courtship flight of white butterflies, probably without realising what she was witnessing:

> Instead of rambling vaguely the white butterflies danced one above the other, making their white shifting flakes the outline of a shattered marble column above the flowers.[21]

This was written in Kew Gardens, but the following lines describe the bitter waters of Babylon – Zion distant and fair. Exceptionally, here the spirit and the soul are bracketed.

> Times desolate ages
> Shall still find thee waiting
> For quick fish to rise there,

Love

Or butterfly wooing,
Or flower's honeyed beauty,
Or wood-pigeon cooing.[22]

Pablo Neruda links butterflies and sensual delights:

My sombre heart searches for you nevertheless
and I love your joyful body, your slender and flowing voice.
Dark butterfly, sweet and definitive
like the wheatfield and the sun, the poppy and the water[23]

Most poetry about butterflies seems virtually untranslatable and Heine's verse becomes doggerel in English:

But everyone love I:
The rose, the nightingale, sun's sweet ray.
The evening star, the butterfly.[24]

But some doggerel is agreeable:

O butterfly on whose light wings
The golden summer sunshine clings;
O moon and sun that beam and burn, –
Keep safe my Love till I return![25]

Originally I had intended to confine this anthology to butterflies and exclude moths. But then I realised that the Greeks and the Romans made no difference between the two and their *psyche* and *papilio* cover both. I am glad I decided to include moths, for they, and the angelic butterflies, engender different sentiments with both pen and brush – the sun and the moon. But they are linked to our love rather than their own.

The Soul
The Ancients held that if you saw
A dying man, and watched him breathe
His last, a trembling moth as white as snow
Would glide from out his mouth and float
Into the thinning air.

And when the curtains billow in the dark,
On warm and gentle summer nights,
I have been close enough to you to feel
The moth brush lightly past my face;
And once with a long tender kiss,
I drew her in.[26]

Again:

> Dark Grey moth
> A gleaming spot on each of your wings,
> relaxing in the shadow of the lamp,
> through my window you came flying
> from the cool regions of the night
> where the great stars pulse.
>
> The spots on the wings stare full of reproach
> like the narrow eyes in an African mask.
>
> Whose emissary are you?
> Can I guess? Do I know?
> The emissary of one
> Who has long ceased to come
> But who speaks to me
> through you,
> and all at once through every object in this small room
> through every star in this April night.[27]

Although Patric Dickinson's verse is beside my point, it expresses a relevant emotion – of air and angels and love and white butterflies – rather skilfully.

> I am not a poet who can set
> This beauty like a butterfly
> Upon a jewelled board of rhyme,
> For when I raise love's clumsy net
> I startle wings into the sky
> Up stairs of air I cannot climb.[28]

The Life Spirit

34

To My Anonymous Collaborator

This is a crazy compilation, because we put things on paper carelessly, when we come across them or were spurred on by some chance episode. It was casual and haphazard and unplanned – but whether the quotations are good or bad, or apposite or nonsensical, they seemed to say something at the time, which put salt on the tail of some fleeting but delicious juxtaposition that we both liked. 'Both liked' is of course the only unifying thread in the whole uneven conglomeration. For instance, we discovered that each of us had been delighted that the dove rejected the Ark, and, unlike the proverbial homing pigeon, did not return the moment she could find somewhere else to rest her feet. That episode in Genesis possibly initiated my life-long affection for these beautiful and successful birds, and explains why we have overloaded our text with illustrations by Picasso, for – as we have pointed out already – no-one before or since has, or in a dim and distant future, will ever again understand doves as he did. Not only those scruffy, wanton pigeons in the town square, but the snowy air-and-angel birds chipped out of an azure sky, and those with feathered feet aflame with rainbowed Holy Spirit.

Then, of course, we engendered arguments. For instance, in the chapter on Love I would have liked to fit in Mary Barnard's translation of Sappho's letter to a soldier's wife, but as you pointed out with raised eyebrows, it had nothing whatsoever to do with doves or butterflies – although I insisted, quite unreasonably, they could well be substituted, with a little imagination, for oars and swords.

> Some say a cavalry corps,
> Some infantry, and some again
> Will maintain that the swift oars
>
> Of our fleet are the finest
> Sight on dark earth; but I say
> Whatever one loves, is.[1]

There was another piece of poetry I longed to include because time and again a bird or a butterfly has restored my good humour, but I failed to justify such an inclusion.

> The way a crow
> Shook down on me
> The dust of snow
> From a hemlock tree
>
> Has given my heart
> A change of mood
> And saved some part
> Of a day I had rued[2]

186

La Parole

Finally I tried to add a wildly romantic Magritte – 'La Parole' – a night sky combining the edge of the spirit and the soul. My collaborator, wishing to be conciliatory, admitted yes, it was almost one of her favourites, but how could you justify the inclusion of a picture nowhere connected, even remotely, with the insect or bird world?

I expostulated. 'But if you look long enough you can always find a Dove in Magritte . . .' Of course you were right, but I have included it here all the same. . . .

As a child you were once offered a pet as a reward – or possibly a bribe – for good behaviour before and after tonsillectomy. A puppy? A kitten? A long-haired guinea pig? No. You opted for a dragon. For you can't tame a dragon, or humiliate a dragon by shutting it up in a hutch or by spanking it for territory-marking in the drawing room. Later on we both lit candles to our own curious dragons. I, for one, chose a speck of blue speedwell in preference to a six-foot lapis lazuli garden-grown larkspur, and you were more adventurous and put a match to the tallow on the Silk Road.

You cannot tame butterflies any more than dragons. Suddenly a Brimstone is there, flapping in cool spring sunshine. All the breathtaking scents seem to be wafted towards us with each wing beat – hazel catkins, warm turf, white violets, a haze of bright green caught in the branches of the larch trees, and a tinge of hormone-engendered grace in the air. It is a mystery of which the Brimstone is the symbol – of what? The freedom of the Soul and the Spirit?

Yes, perhaps – but we do not really know. We never really will know.

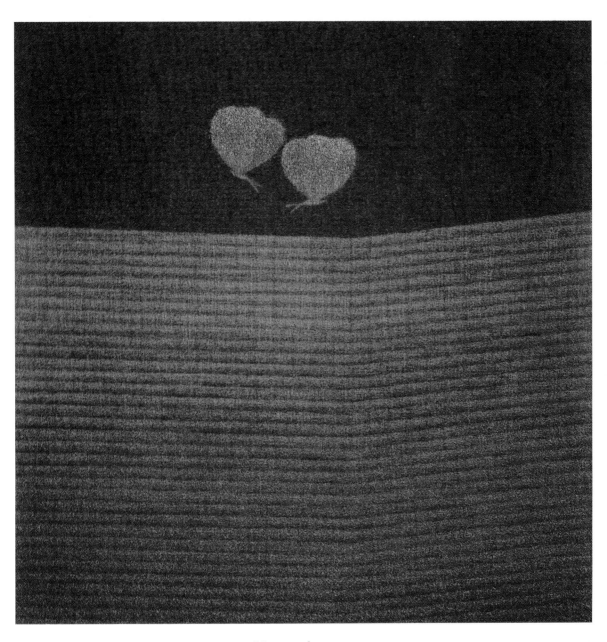

Hormonal grace

Taste is very very odd

Taste

Taste is very, very odd. It is unquestionably a gift from the God who shuffles our genes. You are born with it, and the taste one may *acquire*, with erudition and instruction and practice, is not the genuine article, even though it may form a useful substitute. Fashions come and go, and to a lesser or greater extent form our opinions and influence our likes and dislikes, but taste is just as evident and independent and unambiguous when Greek or Roman marbles are in vogue, or when Monet's water-lilies take the world by storm.

Curiously enough, we can recognise when our complexions are sallow, our legs bandy, and our hair lacklustre and wispy, but we rarely believe we are without artistic sensibility or taste. On the other hand, we are able to recognise the dearth of this quality in not a few of our acquaintances and friends. There are, however, some rare individuals who realise that they have neither taste nor flair and will routinely fail to appreciate either pictures or styles destined to be recognised as works of art or distinguished art-forms in the future. This is strangely disconcerting – but what is taste?

Soule's dictionary of synonyms tells us – among other things – that taste signifies 'the test by the tongue,' to savour and to relish, but in another sense to have perception, experience, discernment of beauty and excellence, and to have judgement of propriety. The Oxford dictionary considers that taste is the mental perception of quality and a discriminating faculty – the sense of what is appropriate, harmonious and beautiful; the discernment, appreciation and enjoyment of what is excellent in art, literature, and nature. (It must also be remembered that in the French language *gout* is used in both senses, in an identical manner. Presumably the most sustained pleasure known to man is eating and tasting simultaneously.) These are fine phrases but curiously enough they seem inadequate and somehow miss the point. They fail to convey the subtle essence of taste, the sureness of touch yet lightness of tone, and the untutored, sensual combination of intuition and experience.

The evolution of taste is also very strange, and the chronological changes experienced by a sophisticated individual will appear to recapitulate the development which has occurred in the population as a whole, over many decades.

The naïve, charming taste of young children is all too frequently dissipated at puberty and we are confused and puzzled by the grip of hor-mones upon our sensibility and understanding. In old age our feeling and taste for poetry dwindles or even deserts us. *The Oxford Book of English Verse* may stir up vague and agreeable memories of the past (Ah, let us be true to one another . . .) but on the whole the over-sixties turn instinc-tively to biography, puzzled by the fact that poetry has somehow lost its savour and become almost incomprehensible.

Doves and butterflies are wonderful yardsticks for taste – they distil the essence out of natural beauty and the poetry of life. Just because of their ageless allure and universal attraction, they are the centre of some of the most excruciatingly tasteless writing and painting ever consigned to paper and canvas. Their appeal to the masses has made them prime favourites for numerous advertisements – for travel, jewellery, night-clubs, cigarettes, books, underwear, beds, exhibitions, light fittings, condoms. The exuberant vulgarity of some of this 'art' has a certain undeniable attraction. Bad taste can be more interesting than good. . . .

We have had to select for our Appendix only a few pictures from several hundred examples – a difficult task – but the illustrations and verses chosen will, we hope, speak for themselves – perhaps elicit mild, ribald laughter but also demonstrate that taste is, indeed, very, very odd.

Morphos

Summer Butterflies

No comment

June Goodfield

PLAYING
GOD

Genetic Engineering
and the Manipulation
of Life

ABACUS

Playing God

April 17, 1971 · THE NEW YORKER · Price 50 cents

'*Not for one moment handsome aged Walt Whitman have I ceased to see your beard full of butterflies*' [1]

trying to break into an electric light bulb

When curiosity flourishes, worlds can be changed.

Why? How? What if? Young people question. Taking joy in the search for solutions. Their worlds abound with endless possibilities. So, too, it is with scientists. Whose laboratories are as limitless as the universe. Whose ideas shape worlds. To interest young minds in the wonders of science, Phillips Petroleum has made possible a film series called "The Search for Solutions." Stimulating films aired on PBS and seen by over two million students per month. They capture the excitement of discovery. And the discoverer. To teach. To encourage. But most of all, to interest. Because childlike curiosity in the right hands can help turn darkness into light.

Wonder

Silk Cut

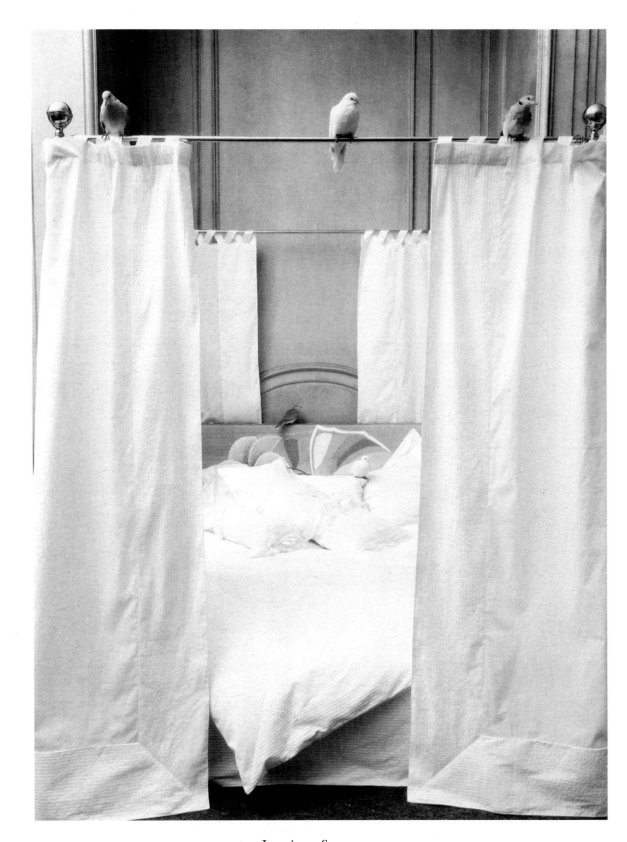

Luminous Summer

Mike Tyson holding a Dove

REFERENCES

1 · THE SOUL

1 Pablo Neruda. *Twenty Love Poems and a Song of Despair*.
2 Genesis 2:7.
3 John Masefield. 'The Chief Centurions', from *The Tragedy of Pompey the Great*.
4 Aristotle. *Aristotle's De Anima*. Books II, III, trans. by D. W. Hamlyn.
5 Aristotle. *On the Soul*. Books III, VIII, trans. by W. S. Hett.
6 Alfred Tennyson. 'St. Simeon Stylites'.

2 · THE SPIRIT

1 Mark 1:10.
2 Andrew Samuels. *Jung and the Post-Jungians*.
3 Genesis 8:12.
4 Song of Solomon, 2:14.
5 Psalms 68:13.
6 Richard Southwood. 'Entomology and Mankind', *American Scientist*, Vol. 63, 1977.
7 William Shakespeare. *Henry IV, Part II*, Act IV, Scene 1.
8 Bruno Bettelheim. *Freud and Man's Soul*.

3 · LOVE OF THINGS WINGED

1 Victor Hugo. 'Amour des Choses Ailées'.
2 William Cowper. *The Task*, Book IV.
3 John Donne. 'Aire and Angels'.
4 Psalms 55:6.
5 Psalms 55:7.
6 Issa. From *Spring: A History of Haiku*, Vol. II, R. H. Blyth.
7 Walter de la Mare. 'On the Esplanade' (*The Fleeting and Other Poems*).
8 Wording inspired by McDonald's 'The Bonny, Bonny Dell' (cited by S. H. Scudder, *The Butterflies of the Eastern United States and Canada*).
9 Robert Graves. 'Flying Crooked'.
10 Wording inspired by Algernon Charles Swinburne. 'Envoi' (*A Century of Roundels*).
11 A. N. Didron. *Christian Iconography*, Vol. II.
12 Li Shang-Yin. *Poems of the Late T'Ang*, trans. A. C. Graham.
13 Kokku. W. H. Edmonds. *Pointers and Clues in Japanese and Chinese Art*.

4 · SKY-FLAKES

1 Robert Frost. 'Blue Butterfly Day'.
2 Maurice Thompson. 'In Haunts of Bass and Bream' (cited by Scudder).
3 Robert Frost. 'Fragmentary Blue'.
4 Robert Frost. 'Blue Butterfly Day'.
5 Rudyard Kipling. 'Pagett M.P.'
6 Elizabeth Barrett Browning. 'Aurora Leigh'.
7 Charles Marie Leconte de Lisle. 'L'Homme des Champs'.
8 John Milton. *Paradise Lost*, 7:476.
9 John Keats. 'Calidora'.
10 Robert Browning. *The Ring and the Book*.
11 Pablo Neruda. *Cartas de Amor a Albertina*.
12 The Upanishads, trans. Alistair Shearer and Peter Russell.
13 Heinrich Heine. *Lass ab*.
14 Alfred de Vigny. 'Les Papillons'.
15 *Poems of the Late T'ang*, trans. A. C. Graham.
16 Irene Nicholson, trans. *Firefly in the Night: A Study of Ancient Mexican Poetry and Symbolism*.
17 Irene Nicholson, trans. *Firefly in the Night: A Study of Ancient Mexican Poetry and Symbolism*.
18 *Encyclopaedia de Mexico*, Vol. VIII, Mariposas.

5 · ROSES AND BUTTERFLIES

1 Caroline Gilman. 'Child's Wish in June'.
2 John Keats. 'Sleep and Poetry'.
3 W. B. Yeats. 'Another Song of a Fool'.
4 Heinrich Heine. 'A New Spring, No .7', trans. Ireland.
5 Wording inspired by Charles Augustin Sainte-Beuve. 'Pensée d'Automne'.
6 Victor Baleguer. 'The Chaste Butterfly'.
7 Jean Ingelow. 'A Dead Year', *Poems*, Vol. I.
8 Alphonse de Lamartine. 'Le Papillon'.
9 Virginia Woolf. *Collected Letters*, Vol. III.
10 Marcel Proust. *Remembrance of Things Past, Swann's Way*, trans. Scott Moncrieff.
11 Wording inspired by William Shakespeare. *Troilus and Cressida*, Act III, Scene 3.
12 Wording inspired by John Keats. *Endymion*, Book I.

6 · CLOTHES MOTHS

1 Book of Common Prayer, Psalm 39:12.
2 Matthew 6:19.
3 Leo Tolstoy. *Anna Karenina*, Part IV, Chapter 5, trans. Rochelle S. Townsend.
4 Walter de la Mare. 'Eureka'.
5 Percy Bysshe Shelley. *A Defence of Poetry*.

7 · THE GARDEN AND YOUR ROOM

1 Federico Gárcía Lorca. 'Consulted'.
2 William Shakespeare. *Venus and Adonis*.
3 John Keats. *Ode to Psyche*.
4 Ivan Alekseevich Bunin, quoted in *Speak Memory* by Vladimir Nabokov.

8 · CANDLES

1 William Shakespeare. *The Merchant of Venice*, Act II, Scene 8.
2 W. B. Yeats. 'Two Years Later'.
3 W. H. Hudson. *Green Mansions*.
4 Christopher Fry. *Venus Observed*, Act II, Scene 2.
5 Pliny. *Natural History*, trans. John Bostock and H. T. Riley, Henry G. Bohn, 1856.
6 Walter de la Mare. 'The Moth'.
7 Don Marquis. *Archy and Mehitabel*.
8 Percy Bysshe Shelley. 'Short Lyric'.
9 James Boswell. *Life of Johnson*.
10 Thomas Hardy. *The Return of the Native*.
11 Luis de Góngora. *Second Solitude* I:8.
12 Vladimir Nabokov. *Glory*, trans. by Dimitri and Vladimir Nabokov.
13 Vladimir Nabokov. *Speak Memory*.
14 Vladimir Nabokov. *Glory*, op. cit.
15 D. J. Enright. 'Some Men Are Brothers'.
16 John Donne. 'Recusancy'.
17 T. S. Eliot. 'Whispers of Immortality'.

9 · VLADIMIR NABOKOV AND THE SMALL GILDED FLY

1 William Shakespeare, *King Lear*, Act IV, Scene 6.
2 Vladimir Nabokov. Review, *Radio Times*.
3 Thomas Browne. *Religio Medici*.
4 Siegfried Sassoon. *The Old Century and Seven More Years*.
5 Boris Pasternak. *Doctor Zhivago*.
6 Robert Browning. *An Englishman in Italy*.
7 Vladimir Nabokov. *Speak Memory*.
8 Vladimir Nabokov. *Speak Memory*.

10 · SILK

1 William Shakespeare, *Othello*, Act III, Scene 4.
2 Robert Herrick. 'Upon Julia's Clothes'.
3 Terence Tiller, 'Epithalamion'.
4 Pliny. *Natural History*, Vol. III.
5 Geoffrey Chaucer. *Canterbury Tales*, 'The Maunciple's Tale'.
6 Ezekiel 16:10.
7 Proverbs 31:22.
8 Walter de la Mare. *Quiet, The Fleeting and Other Poems*.
9 Percy Bysshe Shelley. *Epistle to Maria Gisborne*.
10 John Dryden. *Of the Pythagorean Philosophy*.
11 Erasmus Darwin. *Botanic Garden*.
12 Erasmus Darwin. *The Temple of Nature*.
13 Coventry Patmore. *The Angel in the House*.
14 John Donne. 'The Bait'.
15 Erasmus Darwin. *The Temple of Nature*.
16 William Blake. *Auguries of Innocence*.

11 · ALONG THE SILK ROAD

1 Federico García Lorca. *El Maleficio de la Mariposa*, trans. Carmen Wheatley.
2 Peter Hopkirk. *Foreign Devils on the Silk Road*.
3 Dylan Thomas. *A Prospect of the See. A Story*.
4 Reuven Gagil. *The Desert Camel*.

13 · VAN GOGH AND THE BUTTERFLIES

1 Herder. 'To a Butterfly', trans. J. V. H.
2 Vincent Van Gogh letter 477, 10-14 April, in *Vincent Van Gogh* by J. B. de la Faille.
3 G. D. Blanchard. *A Pilgrimage: Newgate Exercise Yard*.

14 · MARCEL PROUST, NATURALIST

1 William Shakespeare. *Venus and Adonis*.
2 William Shakespeare. *Romeo and Juliet*, Act I, Scene 5.
3 Marcel Proust. *Remembrance of Things Past. Swann's Way, Place-Names. The Name*.
4 Ibid. *Swann's Way, Cambray*.
5 Ibid. *Swann's Way, Cambray*.
6 Ibid. *Within a Budding Grove*.
7 Ibid. *The Guermantes Way*.
8 Ibid. *The Captive*.
9 Ibid. *The Captive*.
10 Ibid. *The Captive*.
11 Ibid. *The Captive*.
12 Ibid. *Swann's Way, Cambray*.

15 · NERUDA AND THE BUTTERFLY OF SHADOW

1 Pablo Neruda. 'Little America'.
2 Pablo Neruda. *Cartas de Amor a Albertina*.
3 Pablo Neruda. 'Angel Cruchaga'.
4 Pablo Neruda. *Cartas de Amor a Albertina*.
5 William Blake. *The Marriage of Heaven and Hell*.
6 Pablo Neruda. 'The White Bee'.

16 · HUNTING BUTTERFLIES

1 Ben Jonson. 'To a Friend: An Epigramme of Inigo Jones'.
2 William Drummond. 'The Happiness of a Flea', from *Madrigalles and Epigrammes*.
3 John Donne. 'The Flea'.
4 John Donne. 'The Flea'.
5 Samuel I 26:13.
6 Samuel I 26:20.
7 William Hazlitt. *On Thought and Action*.
8 Egyptian, XVIIIth Dynasty. 'Fowling in the Marshes', British Museum.
9 John Bunyan. From *Oxford Book of Children's Verse*.
10 Geoffrey Chaucer. *The Works of Chaucer*.
11 H. H. Tomlinson. *Sea and the Jungle*.
12 Alfred Russel Wallace. Chapter by Patrick Matthews from *The Pursuit of Moths and Butterflies*.
13 William Shakespeare. *Coriolanus*, Act I, Scene 3.
14 Alexander Pope. *The Dunciad* (B), Book IV.
15 Dimitri Nabokov. *Vladimir Nabokov*.
16 Virginia Woolf. 'Reading'. *The Captain's Death-Bed and other Essays*.
17 Evelyn Cheesman. *From the Land of the Red Bird*.
18 William Shakespeare. *Antony and Cleopatra*, Act I, Scene 4.
19 Anonymous.

17 · YELLOW BUTTERFLIES

1 Anonymous.
2 Frederic Prokosch. *Voices: A Memoir*.
3 Vladimir Nabokov. *Speak, Memory*.
4 George Wald. *The Distribution and Evolution of Visual Systems*.
5 Jeremiah 14:6.
6 Robert Gittings. *Villa in the South*.
7 W. W. Story. 'Under the Ilexes'.
8 Nina Epton. *Islands of the Sunbird*.
9 Gérard de Nerval. From *Butterflies of New England* by S. H. Scudder, 1889.
10 Marcel Proust. *The Cities of the Plain*.

11 Peter Russell. 'Missing a Bus'.
12 Oscar Wilde. 'Symphony in Yellow'.
13 Leonard Cohen. 'After the Sabbath Prayers'.
14 Gabriel García Márquez. *One Hundred Years of Solitude*, translated from the Spanish, 1969, by Carmen Wheatley.
15 Irene Nicholson. *Firefly in the Night*.
16 Pablo Neruda. 'Every Day You Play'.

18 · THE WINGED CONJUNCTION

1 Robert Gittings. 'A Breath of Air'.
2 John Donne. 'The Canonisation'.
3 Pablo Neruda. 'I Like for You to Be Still'.
4 Lewis Belrose. 'Mid-Summer'.
5 Sappho. 'Ode to Aphrodite', trans. M. Barnard.

19 · CAPTIVE SPIRITS

1 William Shakespeare, *Romeo and Juliet*, Act I, Scene 3.
2 Isaiah 60:8.
3 Matthew 21:12.
4 John 2:16.
5 Charles Darwin. *The Origin of Species*.
6 V. Sackville-West. 'Nostalgia' *Collected Poems*.
7 William Blake. *Auguries of Innocence*.
8 Kyoko. *An Anthology of Haiku Ancient and Modern*, trans. Asataro Miyamaric.
9 Wendell Levi. 'The Pigeon'.
10 William Shakespeare. *As You Like It*, Act IV, Scene 1.
11 William Shakespeare. *Romeo and Juliet*, Act II, Scene 5.
12 Gerard Manley Hopkins. *Journal*, June 16, 1873.
13 Peter Levi. *Notebook*. 'Homage to Brancusi'.
14 Dante Gabriel Rossetti. 'Sunset Wings'.

20 · SWEET LITTLE RED FEET! WHY DID YOU DIE?

1 John Keats. 'A Song'.
2 W. H. Davies. 'Birds'.
3 David R. Jones and Kjell Johansen. *The Blood Vascular System of Birds. Avian Biology*, Vol. II.
4 Kenneth Patchen. 'Pastoral'.
5 Christopher Fry. *The Lady's Not for Burning*.
6 Alfred Tennyson. 'The Princess'.
7 Walter de la Mare. 'The Dove'.
8 Hugh of St. Victor. *De Bestris et Allis Rebus*, Book 1.

21 · THE WHITE FANTAILS

1 Ovid. *Metamorphosis*, trans. Joseph Addison.
2 E. O. Wilson. *On Human Nature*.
3 Anonymous.

22 · WHEN THAT HER GOLDEN COUPLETS
  ARE DISCLOS'D

1 William Shakespeare. *Hamlet*, Act V, Scene 1.

23 · PICASSO AND HIS DOVES

1 Izaak Walton. 'The Angler's Wish'.
2 Françoise Gilot. *Life with Picasso*.

24 · MARY AND THE DOVE

1 John Milton. *Paradise Lost* I, 20-23.
2 John 1:32.
3 Peter Levi. *Monologue Spoken by the Pet Canary of Pope Pius XII*.
4 Gerard Manley Hopkins. 'God's Grandeur'.
5 Guillaume Apollinaire. *Le Bestiaire ou Cortège d'Orphée*, trans. Jean Wood.

25 · MILK

1 John Donne. An 'Epithalamion' or Marriage Song: On the Lady Elizabeth and Count Palatine being married on St. Valentine's Day, 1613.

26 · RAINBOW BUTTERFLIES AND AMOROUS
  DOVES

1 Rabindranath Tagore. 'Fireflies'.
2 S. H. Scudder. *Butterflies of New England*, Vol. II.
3 Geoffrey Chaucer. 'The Nun's Priest's Tale'.
4 Samuel Taylor Coleridge. 'Psyche'.
5 J. C. Cooper. *Encyclopaedia of Traditional Symbols*.
6 Ibid.
7 C. A. S. Williams. 'Outline of Chinese Symbolism', quoted from the book of Odes.
8 Jean de Boschère.
9 James Thomson. 'Spring'.
10 Iris Murdoch. *The Black Prince*.
11 John Milton. 'On the Morning of Christ's Nativity' (1629).
12 James Montgomery. 'Pelican Island'.
13 Salvatore Quasimodo. 'Piazza Fontana'.

27 · VALLEY OF THE BUTTERFLIES

1 T. W. Higginson. 'Ode to a Butterfly'.
2 William Shakespeare. *King Lear*, Act IV, Scene 6.

29 · DREAMS

1 William Cowper. *The Task*, Book III, 'The Garden'.
2 Thomas Hardy.
3 Thomas Hardy. 'Friends Beyond'.
4 Peter Levi. 'Portrait'.
5 Walter de la Mare. 'The Burning Glass'.
6 Virginia Woolf. *Collected Essays*. 'Reading'.
7 Roy Fuller. 'Letter to My Wife'.
8 W. J. Turner. 'In Time Like Glass'.
9 Gerard Manley Hopkins. *The Poems of Epithalamion*, 4th ed.
10 Samuel Palmer.
11 Chuang-tzu, trans. from Gweneth and Bernard Johnston, *This Is Hong Kong: Butterflies*.

30 · DISASTERS

1 Leonard Cohen. 'For Wilf and His House'.
2 Alexander Pope. 'Epistle to Dr. Arbuthnot'.
3 Matthew Arnold. 'The Light of Asia'.
4 John Keats. 'Endymion'.
5 Virgil. *Aeneid*, Book I, trans. Dryden.
6 Edmund Spenser. 'The Shepherd's Calendar'.
7 Alexander Pope. 'Windsor Forest'.
8 Alexander Pope. 'Duke on the Death of Charles II'.
9 Herbert Read. 'The Falcon and the Dove'.
10 J. J. Audubon. *Ornithological Biography*, Vol. II.
11 Bernard Lazare. *Le Fumier de Job*.
12 Leviticus 1:15-17.
13 Luke 2:21-24.
14 John Donne. *Sermons*. 'Meditation 12'.
15 Samuel Pepys. *Diary*, October 19, 1663.
16 Isaiah 59:11.
17 Alfred Tennyson. 'The Miller's Daughter'.
18 Stevie Smith. 'The Old Sweet Dove of Wiveton'.
19 Robert Gittings. 'Blizzard'.
20 Virginia Woolf. *To the Lighthouse*.
21 Leonard Cohen. 'Inquiry into the Nature of Cruelty'.
22 Federico García Lorca. 'After the Walk', trans. Carmen Wheatley.
23 Percy Bysshe Shelley. 'The Witch of Atlas'.
24 Anonymous.
25 Pablo Neruda. 'Ode with a Lament', concluding verse.
26 Erich Maria Remarque. *All Quiet on the Western Front*.
27 Victor Hugo. *Les Misérables*, Pt. 5.

31 · MIGRATION

1 Hosea 11:11.
2 Moero. 'The Childhood of Zeus', trans. T. F. Higham.
3 Wording inspired by Alfred Tennyson. 'The Eagle'.
4 Robin Baker. *Animal Migration*.
5 John Milton. 'Lycidas'.
6 Julian Bell. 'The Redshanks'.
7 Pliny. *Natural History*, Vol. II, trans. Bostock and Riley.
8 Strabo.
9 Wendell Levi. 'The Pigeon'.
10 Edith Thomas. 'August'.
11 Anonymous. 'A Stalker of Geese', trans. William Morris.

32 · SORROW

1 William Shakespeare. *Othello*, Act I, Scene 3.
2 John Drinkwater. 'Lord Rameses of Egypt sighed . . .'.
3 William Browne. 'Memory'.
4 Salvatore Quasimodo.
5 Percy Bysshe Shelley. 'Epipsychidion'.
6 Angelo de Costanzo. 'Sonnet', trans. Carmen Wheatley.
7 Victor Hugo. 'La Tristesse'.
8 Padraic Colum. 'No Child'.
9 Wallace Stevens. 'Song of Fixed Accord'.
10 Dimitri Nabokov. trans. Peter Quennell. *Vladimir Nabokov, His Life, His Work, His World*.
11 Heinrich Heine. *Lass ab*.

33 · LOVE

1 William Shakespeare. *Venus and Adonis*.
2 John Donne. *Sermons*, 'Christmas Day'.
3 Wendell Levi. 'The Pigeon'.
4 G. L. L. Buffon. *Le Pigeon*.
5 Edward Herbert, Lord Cherbury. 'Kissing'.
6 Gilbert White. *Letters* XLII to the Hon. Daines Barrington.
7 J. Moore. 'Columbarium and the Pigeon House'.
8 Peter Levi. Good Friday Sermon.
9 Luis de Góngora. 'Polyphemus and Galatea', trans. Gilbert Cunningham.
10 Sir Philip Sidney. *Astrophel and Stella*.
11 D. D. Moffat. 'Complaint of Nature'.
12 Walter de la Mare. *The Burning Glass and Other Poems*.
13 Song of Solomon 1:15.
14 Ibid. 4:1.
15 Petrarch (of Laura). *Rime Sparse*.
16 Robert Browning. 'Love in the Campagna'.
17 Alfred Tennyson. 'Maud'
18 Victor Hugo. *Les Misérables*.
19 T. S. Eliot. 'Little Gidding'.
20 William Shakespeare *Troilus and Cressida*, Act III, Scene 1.
21 Virginia Woolf. 'Kew Gardens'.
22 Walter de la Mare. 'Bitter Waters'.
23 Pablo Neruda. *Twenty Love Poems and a Song of Despair*.
24 Heinrich Heine. *Lass ab*.
25 R. W. Gilder. 'Sweet Wild Rose'.
26 Anonymous.
27 David Gill. 'Moth'.
28 Patric Dickinson.

34 · TO MY ANONYMOUS COLLABORATOR

1 Sappho. 'Love Song to Anactoria'; a new translation by Mary Barnard, University of California Press, Berkeley, Calif., 1958.
2 Robert Frost. 'Dust of Snow'.

APPENDIX

1 Concha Lorca. 'Oda a Walt Whitman'.

ACKNOWLEDGEMENTS

The following authors and publishers kindly gave us permission to reprint whole poems or extracts from their work:

Anvil Press Poetry Limited: 'Monologue Spoken by the Pet Canary of Pope Pius XII', 'Notebook/ Homage to Brancusi' and 'Good Friday Sermon 1972' from Peter Levi *Collected Poems*.

Dorothy Bailey: H M Tomlinson *The Sea and the Jungle*.

The Bodley Head: Jean de Bosschere *Job le Pauvre*; Erich Maria Remarque *All Quiet on the Western Front*.

Jonathan Cape: Robert Frost 'Blue Butterfly Day' from *Fragmentary Blue*; 'Dust of Snow' from *The Poetry of Robert Frost*; Leonard Cohen 'Inquiry into the Nature of Cruelty' and 'For Wilf and his House' from *Selected Poems*, 'After Sabbath Prayers' from *The Spice Box of the Earth*; W H Davies 'Birds' from *The Poems*; Gabriel García Márquez *One Hundred Years of Solitude* (translated Gregory Rabassa); Pablo Neruda *Twenty Love Poems and a Song of Despair* (translated W S Merwin) and 'Ode with a Lament' from *Selected Poems* ed. Nathaniel Tarn.

Chatto & Windus and The Hogarth Press: Bruno Bettelheim *Freud and Man's Soul*; Iris Murdoch *The Black Prince*; Julian Bell *The Redshanks*.

Faber & Faber: T S Eliot *Four Quartets*; Frederick Prokosch *Voices, a Memoir*; Irene Nicholson *Firefly in the Night, A Study of Ancient Mexican Poetry and Symbolism*; Wallace Stevens *Collected Poems*.

Farrar, Straus & Giroux: Joseph Brodsky 'The Butterfly' *A Part of Speech*; Salvatore Quasimodo *Piazza Fontana*; Frederick Prokosch *Voices, a Memoir*.

Robert Gittings: 'Blizzard' and 'A Breath of Air'.

Harcourt Brace Jovanovich: T S Eliot 'Little Gidding' *Four Quartets*; Virginia Woolf *To the Lighthouse*; Virginia Woolf *Collected Letters* and 'Reading' from *The Captain's Deathbed and Other Essays*.

Harper & Row Publishers Inc: Gabriel García Márquez *One Hundred Years of Solitude* (translated Gregory Rabassa).

Harvard University Press: Edward O Wilson *On Human Nature*, copyright © 1978 the President and Fellows of Harvard College reprinted by permission of the Harvard University Press, Cambridge, Mass.

David Higham: Herbert Read *The Falcon and the Dove*.

Hodder & Stoughton: Robin Baker *The Evolutionary Ecology of Animal Migration*.

The Hogarth Press and the Executors of the Virginia Woolf Estate: Virginia Woolf *To the Lighthouse*; *Collected Letters*; 'Reading' from *The Captain's Deathbed and Other Essays*.

Henry Holt & Company Inc: Robert Frost 'Blue Butterfly Day', copyright © 1923 Holt Rinehard & Winston, renewed 1951; 'Dust of Snow' *The Poetry of Robert Frost*, ed. Edward Connery Latham.

International Thompson Publishing & Routledge: Andrew Samuels *Jung and the Post Jungians*; Nina Epton 'Islands of the Sunbird' from Patrick Matthews *Pursuit of Moths and Butterflies*.

Alfred A Knopf Inc: Bruno Bettelheim *Freud and Man's Soul*, copyright © 1982; 'Song of Fixed Accord' from *The Collected Poems of Wallace Stevens*, copyright © 1952.

Library of Congress: *An Anthology of Haiku Ancient and Modern* (translated Asataro Miyamori).

Macmillan Publishing: Leonard Cohen 'Inquiry into the Nature of Cruelty' and 'For Wilf and His House' from *Selected Poems*, 'After the Sabbath Prayers' from *The Spice Box of the Earth*; Rabindranath Tagore *Fireflies*.

John Murray & The University of Massachussets Press: Peter Hopkirk *Foreign Devils on the Silk Road*.

New Directions Publishing Corporation: Stevie Smith 'The Old Sweet Dove of Wiveton' from *Collected Poems*, copyright © 1972.

Nigel Nicolson: Vita Sackville-West 'Nostalgia' from *Collected Poems*.

Mrs M O'Sullivan on behalf of the Estate: Padraic Colum *No Child* (Macmillan).

Oxford University Press: Robert Graves 'Flying Crooked' from *Collected Poems*.

Penguin Books: Li Shang-Yin 'To Tzu-chih: among the Flowers' and 'The Patterned Lute' from *Poems of the Late T'Ang* (translated A C Graham); Salvatore Quasimodo 'Piazza Fontana' from *Selected Poems*; H M Tomlinson *The Sea and the Jungle*.

Penguin Modern Classics: 'The Old Sweet Dove of Wiveton' *The Collected Poems of Stevie Smith*.

Laurence Pollinger: Françoise Gilot *Life with Picasso*.

Random House, USA: Vladimir Nabakov *Speak Memory, Glory*; *Vladimir Nabakov: his Life, his Work, his World* ed. Peter Quennell.

Secker & Warberg: Roy Fuller 'Letter to my Wife' from *New and Collected Poems 1934-1984*.

Sidgwick & Jackson: W J Turner *In Time Like Glass*.

The Society of Authors, being the Literary Trustees of Walter de la Mare: 'Bitter Waters', 'The Moth', 'Quiet', 'On the Esplanade' and 'The Dove'.

University of California Press: ed. Mary Bernard 'Love Song by Sappho to Anactoria' from *Sappho: A New Translation*.

Viking Press: Pablo Neruda *Twenty Love Poems and a Song of Despair*, 'Ode with a Lament' from *Selected Poems*.

Watkins Loomis Agency: Françoise Gilot *Life with Picasso*.

A P Watt on behalf of the Executors of the Estate: Robert Graves 'Flying Crooked' from *Collected Poems*.

Weidenfeld & Nicolson: Vladimir Nabakov *Speak Memory, Glory*; *Vladimir Nabakov: His Life, His Work, His World* ed. Peter Quennell.

We also obtained permission to reproduce pictures, drawings and photographs from the following sources:

American Museum of Natural History, New York; Ashmolean Museum, Oxford; Barcelona Cathedral; Stanley Batkin; Biologie in Uusererzeit; Bodleian Library, Oxford; Borghese Gallery, Rome; Brazilian Art Gallery; Debret, Paris; British Library; Trustees of the British Museum; Chester Beatty Library, Dublin; Christie's, London and New York; S Clemente, Rome; Courturier Galleries, Connecticut; The Detroit Institute of Arts; Edita, Lausanne; Galerie Ditesheim; Gallerie de France et Benelux; Georgia Museum of Art; Glasgow Museums and Art Galleries; The Burrell Collection; Japanese Imperial Palace; Kawabata Ryushi Memorial Museum, Tokyo; Kirkpatrick Cards; Maison Française, Paris; Medici Gallery, London; Metropolitan Museum of Art, New York; Musée des Beaux Arts, Lille; Musée National du Château de Fontainbleau; Musée Picasso, Paris; Museum of Fine Arts, Boston; Naples Museum; National Gallery, London; Naturwissenschafliche, Stuttgart; The New Yorker Magazine; Pierre Matisse Gallery, New York; Portal Gallery, London; Prado Museum, Madrid; Pushkin State Museum of Fine Arts, Moscow; John Rylands Library, Manchester; Sotheby's, London and New York; Sphere Books; Tate Gallery, London; Victoria and Albert Museum, London; Vincent Van Gogh Foundation, National Museum; Vincent Van Gogh, Amsterdam.

To all those we express our warmest thanks. We would also like to express our appreciation for a few pictures and quotations for which we failed, despite every effort, to trace the authorship.

INDEX

The bracketed numbers that follow some page references are note numbers. These have been included when the subject is named in the note but not in the main text. Page references in *italic* type indicate illustrations.